GOD'S PROMISE

GOD'S PROMISE

COVENANT RELATIONSHIP IN JOHN

SHERRI BROWN

Paulist Press
New York / Mahwah, NJ

Cover image by Samazur / Shutterstock.com
Cover and book design by Lynn Else

Library of Congress Cataloging-in-Publication Data:

Brown, Sherri.
    God's promise : covenant relationship in John / Sherri Brown.
        pages cm
    Includes bibliographical references.
    ISBN 978-0-8091-4899-8 (pbk. : alk. paper) — ISBN 978-1-58768-423-4 (ebook)
    1. Covenants—Biblical teaching. 2. Bible. John—Criticism, interpretation, etc. 3. Bible. Epistles of John—Criticism, interpretation, etc. 4. Bible. John—Textbooks. 5. Bible. Epistles of John—Textbooks. I. Title.
    BS2601.B78 2014
    231.7`6—dc23

                                                                    2014012786

ISBN 978-0-8091-4899-8 (paperback)
ISBN 978-1-58768-423-4 (e-book)

Published by Paulist Press
997 MacArthur Boulevard
Mahwah, New Jersey 07430

www.paulistpress.com

Printed and bound in the
United States of America

To my father, Patrick Henry Brown III,
and to my *doctor-father*, Francis J. Moloney, SDB.
Thank you.

For just as from the heavens the rain and snow come down and do not return there until they have watered the earth, making it bring forth and sprout, giving seed to the sower and bread to the eater, so shall my word be that goes forth from my mouth. It shall not return to me empty, but shall do my will, achieving the end for which I sent it.

—Isaiah 55:10–11

CONTENTS

INTRODUCTION

An often repeated aphorism traditionally attributed to the fourth-century Christian bishop and eventual saint, John Chrysostom, asserts that the Gospel of John is "like a magic pool in which an infant can paddle and an elephant can swim." This Gospel has so much to teach us that we can spend our lives exploring its waters and discovering new depths. But even after just a dip of the toes, we can see that this Evangelist, traditionally called John, has a unique perspective on the good news of Christ. The Gospel itself calls attention to an otherwise unnamed disciple whom Jesus loved, the Beloved Disciple, as the eyewitness authority behind its good news. Further, the Gospel gives evidence that it was written for a particular community undergoing crises that challenged its faith and unity. St. Irenaeus (c. AD 180), is the first to identify this Beloved Disciple as John, the son of Zebedee, one of Jesus' inner circle of disciples, who lived in Ephesus until the time of the Roman Emperor Trajan (c. AD 98). Scholars therefore often refer to John's community as the community of the Beloved Disciple and the literature it produced as the Johannine Literature, including three epistles alongside the Gospel. Our project in this particular swim in the waters of the Johannine Literature is to explore the underlying theme of covenant as the evangelist's teaching of God's promise to humanity. In preparation, we will consider the Bible as the sacred text of Christianity, the role of covenant in this story, and the impetus behind understanding covenant as a force in John's storytelling strategy as he shares his profound experience of the revelation of God through Jesus Christ.

The Sacred Text of Christianity:
The Bible and Covenant with God

The Christian Bible is made up of the Old Testament (OT) and the New Testament (NT). The term *testament* typically means "will." The English word comes from the Latin *testamentum*, which was used in the first Latin translation of the Bible, the Vulgate. This Latin term translates the Greek word *diathēkē* used in the earliest Christian writings, which itself is a translation of the Hebrew word *berit*, meaning "covenant." In the Jewish Scriptures, the term "covenant" often refers to agreements initiated and spelled out by God, thus "a God-given relationship with mutual commitments." This concept of covenant is the principal means by which the Hebrew Scriptures describe the relationship of God to Israel. What the earliest Christians seem to have understood happened in the Christ event is the formation of a "new covenant" between God and humankind. Christians eventually called the collection of writings about their experience the new covenant, or NT. However, we cannot refer to something as "new" without a concept of "old" or understanding another body of literature as the OT. Christians understand God's activity recorded in the NT to be the fulfillment of God's activity as preserved in the OT. The stories of Jesus Christ in the NT are called Gospels, a term that means "good news." But what exactly is the news and why is it good? The good news is that God has fulfilled all his prior covenantal activity in the incarnation and redeeming sacrifice of his Son and put in place a new covenant available to humankind based on faith. This is the story the Gospel writers, the evangelists, share with their communities and all who will hear. The first three Gospels of the NT—Matthew, Mark, and Luke—follow the same general plot and are called the Synoptic Gospels. John's Gospel is so strikingly distinctive that it is often identified as the "Fourth Gospel." Nonetheless, covenant remains a deeply embedded part of the storytelling fabric of John, the Fourth Evangelist.

At its root, a covenant is defined as an agreement enacted between two parties in which one or both make promises under oath to perform or to refrain from performing certain actions stipulated in advance. The OT authors use the metaphor of covenant to express the special relationship between God and God's Creation in general, and God's chosen people Israel in particular. Both the texts that narrate the story of Israel and its relationship with God and the prophetic literature that communicates God's will and summons Israel to live rightly in this relationship are replete with accounts of and references to God's covenantal activity in the world. In addition to detailed recounting of covenant-making and covenant-renewing rituals and ceremonies, this literature preserves the broader imagery and themes of the covenant metaphor. These storytellers and prophets integrate this language into their larger works in order to share their message of life in unique relationship with God, even when the term "covenant" does not appear. The prophets in particular rarely use the word itself, even as they infuse their works with calls to covenant relationship. Likewise, this term does not appear in the Johannine Literature. Nonetheless, like his scriptural predecessors, this Evangelist incorporates the metaphor of covenant in the telling of his message. Without ever using the word itself, the Fourth Evangelist weaves the thematic language and symbolism of covenant throughout his story of God's activity in the world in and through Jesus as a literary technique to draw his readers into his sacred narrative of true relationship with God.

John's Story of God's Covenantal Promise

There has been a gradual uncovering of the important component of covenant as the background to the Johannine writings in biblical scholarship over the past fifty years. At the same time, the landscape of biblical criticism in general has shifted. In recent decades, building upon the acquisitions of historical criticism, the discipline of narrative criticism has emerged in biblical studies as an approach that integrates the historical method with a focus on the final form of the text that preserves its sacred nature. Recent scholarship has therefore begun to reassert an emphasis on the thematic unity and end product of the Fourth Gospel, revealing, among other things, a new paradigm for reading John against the background of covenant. From a narrative perspective, the

Johannine story of Jesus Christ is a carefully crafted theological treatise underpinned by symbolic discourse on covenant and scripture. Through his Gospel and Letters, the Fourth Evangelist provides instruction to a believing community on the nature of its faith in God and God's covenant with Israel. By grasping this theological fabric, the richness of the dialogue and imagery interwoven through John's story is allowed to have its full voice in terms of covenant fulfillment and the ongoing commitment of God to a believing people.

In the present study, we will focus our attention on a broad overview of the Gospel and Letters and bring out this rich storytelling and teaching strategy. Christianity is a covenant between God and humanity. Our biblical authors took this relationship seriously, but also explored its beauty and profundity to make sense of our world and the role we are called to live in it. Chapter 1 presents the OT covenant metaphor, then provides an overview of the story of Israel. In this way both the world of the Fourth Evangelist and the texture of the literary fabric that he used in composing his Gospel story are introduced. Chapter 2 establishes the Prologue (1:1–18) as the gateway to understanding the Gospel. Chapter 3 introduces the Book of Signs, the public ministry of Jesus, beginning with the opening days of the revelation of Jesus that make up the rest of the first chapter (1:19–51), then moving to the journey that teaches readers about believing in the Word of Jesus (John 2—4), before exploring the heart of the ministry as Jesus participates in the feasts of Israel (John 5—10), and concluding with a study of the arrival of the hour of Jesus as he begins to move toward glorification (John 11—12). Chapter 4 introduces the Book of Glory and focuses on Jesus' last discourse with and preparation of his disciples for life and leadership in the new covenant relationship (John 13—17) before presenting the passion narrative focusing on the questions of Christ, kingship, and truth (John 18—19), and concluding with an exploration of the initial resurrection and postresurrection narratives of the Fourth Gospel (John 20). Chapter 5 discusses John 21 as an epilogue to the Gospel that presents the ongoing covenantal dialogue in the community of the church established at the cross. We move into the closing chapters with a look at the Gospel community and its aftermath in the larger early Christian sphere. Chapter 6 studies the three Letters of John as the canonical extension of the community of the Beloved Disciple and the challenges they faced as Christianity grew and developed in an ever-changing world. Finally, a brief conclusion draws together the themes of the book by discussing the covenant and community produced by the Johannine literature in the first century and into the present world.

THE STORY OF ISRAEL

Covenant in Scripture

The introduction suggested that the metaphor of covenant is a means by which the OT authors articulate the special relationship between God and creation in general, and God's chosen people in particular. Biblical scholars disagree about when, in the history of Israel, this idea of covenant developed. For our purposes, since we are interested in what John received as his Scripture, it is best to follow the use of the covenant theme across the story of Israel, as it is recorded in its writings beginning with Genesis and making our way through the narrative books and into the prophets of the OT. Regardless of when these books reached their final form and how the covenants developed, by John's time in the first century, they were read as a continuous narrative of Israel's history in covenant relationship with God. In this chapter, therefore, we will broadly trace the story of Israel in terms of key covenant passages that would have been history for the Fourth Evangelist.

Covenant in the Old Testament

As we read through the OT, a basic component of the covenants between God and human beings emerges: one party of the covenant (God) is vastly more knowledgeable, more powerful, and more "sighted" than the other (humans). In every instance, God *knows*, can *do*, and can *see* things in creation and history that the human parties do not and cannot. This constant feature of the covenantal relationship between God and humankind gives biblical covenants a unique character. God is always the initiating agent of these covenants. This gives God encompassing *authority* in this relationship, while the human participants are always called to some form of *obedience*. There is always a binding of promise and obligation at play. The narrative this relationship produces must be given its due, for this is the story that was alive and binding for the Fourth Evangelist. Therefore, what follows is not close exegesis (technical biblical analysis), but rather a more broadly drawn interpretation of the Scriptures that were intimately known to the Fourth Evangelist because they comprised the integral symbolic and theological components of his first-century Jewish worldview. They told the story of Israel—*his* story—in the order of God's plan for creation. We will thus trace the developing covenantal tradition in the historical order that would have been known to the Evangelist, leaving off at a point in the story where he could have found himself picking it up again.

THE "COVENANT" THROUGH ADAM: GENESIS 1—3

The Book of Genesis can be divided in the broadest sense into two parts. Genesis 1—11 is an account of the primordial history of the known world. The text then moves into the more specific account of the ancestry of the people of Israel with the patriarchal narratives of Genesis 12—50. Several key covenantal texts are narrated across Genesis; we will begin with Genesis 1—3. I have enclosed the term *covenant* in quotation marks in this section heading because the term itself never appears in this passage. Similar to the Gospel of John, what we see in the creation account is the establishment of binding relationships between God and humankind through promises and obligations without specific identification of that relationship. We will discuss this passage here because these initial chapters of Jewish Scripture set the pattern for how God works in the world, how the world itself works, and how humankind is created to respond to God. It is only later that these established relationships are identified as "covenant."

The beginning of Israel's story tells of God's word of creation. God literally spoke creation into being (1:1—2:4a). Communication thus becomes the basis of relationship, and relationship becomes the basis of God's interaction with creation. The seeds of covenantal theology are planted with creation and are manifest in God's people with God's word to Adam (2:16–17). God gives Adam life and food and shelter, then culminates the covenant in the gift of community with the creation of his partner, the woman (2:18–25). In return, God demands obedience. The promises of intimate relationship with God and care for creation as well as the obligation of obedience in refraining from eating from the tree of the knowledge of good and evil is marked by the dwelling place of Eden, where humankind can commune with God "in the evening breeze" (3:8). When Adam and Eve fail through disobedience and the perfect union of that relationship is broken (3:1–24), the reestablishment of right relationship with God becomes the guiding force of the rest of the Jewish Scriptures. Sin and death enter the world through disobedience, and quickly spread as humankind grows (4:1—6:8). The narrative is careful to illustrate, however, that God never breaks fidelity to his promises. Even as Adam and Eve lose their right to Eden, God clothes and prepares them for the life they have chosen (3:21). God begins to rectify this relationship with creation by offering a covenant to Noah.

THE COVENANT THROUGH NOAH: GENESIS 6—9

The story of Noah and his experience of covenant with God makes up Genesis 6—9. Genesis 6 opens with a strange and provocative story of the spread of humankind that is consonant with the multiplication of evil across the earth (6:1–4). Humankind to whom the earth was given and whose inclination was to be for God, focused only on evil. God's heart was aggrieved and he determined to "un-create" through the flood. But Noah found favor in the eyes of God (v. 8), ensuring that "re-creation" would follow.

Noah is characterized immediately as a father who is "righteous," "blameless," and who "walked with God" (vv. 9–10). Because of this character, God chooses to save the best of that already created through Noah. God opens by giving Noah his reasoning and his intent (v. 13), then begins his instruction to Noah by way of an imperative ("Make yourself an ark," vv. 14–16). He then clarifies his plan: "For my part, I am going to bring a flood" to destroy what is on the earth, "but I will establish my covenant

3

with you" (v. 18). The first occurrence of "covenant" (*berit* in Hebrew) in the OT is found here in the mouth of God through his directive to Noah, following with detailed directions for all that Noah must do in order to bring it about. "Noah did this; he did all that God commanded him" (v. 22). Genesis 7—8 details the flood itself as God likewise does as promised, allowing the waters of the deep and the heavens to burst forth. God then begins to speak to Noah again and once more opens with a command, this time "Go out." Noah again responds in full obedience to God's call. This second act of response in action is followed by Noah's first initiating action as he builds an altar and offers a burnt sacrifice. God gives his blessing to Noah as well as an imperative for fertility. The sanctity of life, particularly human life, is affirmed, however limited and transient. Genesis 9 then turns to God's covenant with Noah. What was promised before the flood comes to fruition as part of the re-creative communication. God makes his covenant with Noah and his offspring as well as with all of the re-created order. The covenant is eternal and creation will never again be destroyed by a flood. Noah, the primary human character of this account, is silent throughout. God initiates all the action and does all the speaking. Noah's response is in his obedient action, wherein he accepts God's word of covenant and lives his life in accord with that relationship, thus facilitating God's covenant with all creation.

Genesis 6—9, therefore, tells the story of God's work in creation, beginning anew through Noah. This is ultimately a covenant between God and the created order, and the mark of this covenant is the rainbow (9:12–17). God's covenantal relationship with humankind, however, needs more story as the early chapters of Genesis close with the confusion and scattering of humankind following the attempted construction of the tower of Babel (Gen 11). This scattering symbolizes the radical break in the covenantal relationship between God and humankind as the opposite of the unity for which it was created. The story then moves forward several hundred years by way of a genealogy, further symbolizing this breakdown in the relationship. From this point forward, God will never again walk with his creation in the Garden, or anywhere else for that matter. The distance between God and his creation only grows. The characterization of the fearsome and awesome power of God also expands.

THE COVENANT THROUGH ABRAHAM: GENESIS 12—22

The second part of the Book of Genesis, chapters 12—50, covers the ancestral period of the history of Israel. It begins with a man called Abram, whom God eventually renames Abraham. The Abraham cycle of stories begins at Genesis 12 and runs through Genesis 23. Genesis 12 is traditionally understood to recount the call of Abraham. After several centuries of apparent silence, God calls out to one person: "Now God said to Abram, 'Go...'" (v. 1). And that one person responds, taking his family and all that he owns with him: "So Abram went..." (v. 4). Once again the narrative recounts God's call in terms of command and the chosen one's response in action in terms of precise obedience. And for his obedience he receives the assurance of blessing—a great nation and a great name—along with the covenantal obligation of invoking the name of the Lord in blessing or cursing those he encounters (vv. 2-3). After the radical break with creation at Genesis 11, God chooses to work in terms of individual faith and practice. From this action, we find the new basis for a people of God. In response to God's call in Genesis 12, Abram moves his wife, Sarai, and his nephew, Lot, to Canaan.

Crucial for our study is not only God's covenant of divine commitment to Abraham, but also the journey, of both body and spirit, that is integral to the content and the purpose of that covenantal relationship. In the narrative, God's covenant with Abraham grows as Abraham grows. His movement, therefore, is not only physical but spiritual as well, as he moves from pure response in action accompanied by a faith riddled with doubt to a response in action that is grounded in the fullness of faith. Doubt overtakes Abraham almost immediately as he endangers Sarai, the promised matriarch, to the hands of Pharaoh (12:10-20). This doubt continues to hinder Abraham's faith even as he continues to respond in action. Thus, his is a move from strict obedience to obedience in faith. And this is what is eventually reckoned as righteousness.

In Genesis 13, God once again commands Abraham to go, and Abraham complies. This new act of obedience is followed by Abraham's overwhelming success in rescuing Lot from eastern kings, exemplifying his ability to protect his people and overcome his enemies (14:1–24). The proof of this blessing, and Abraham's acknowledgment of it, brings him to the first full expression of God's covenantal action: the promise of progeny (15:1–6) and land (15:7–21). For the first time in the covenant development of the biblical narrative, the human party responds to God verbally (vv. 2–3). Further, Abraham enters into full dialogue with God by expressing his doubt about God's ability to carry out his promise, given the reality of his age. Even more remarkably, God responds not in anger, but in the openness of relationship in communication, bringing Abraham outside and giving the visual confirmation of the stars as the gauge by which his offspring will be numbered (vv. 4–5). Abraham then takes the first step from mere obedience in action to active obedience in faith when "he believed" God. And here God first credits him with "righteousness" (v. 6).

However, this is not the end of Abraham's journey. The very next chapter describes the doubt that persists when Abraham "hearkened to the voice" of another human being, in this case Sarai (16:2), when he has been called time and again to "hearken to the voice" of God. This leads to strife in the family and the endangerment of Abraham's own child (16:3–6). God must intervene, rectifying the wrong done to Hagar, saving the unborn child, and presenting the child Ishmael with a divine commitment of his own (vv. 7–16). God then goes to Abraham and recommits them both to the covenanted promises. Scholars generally consider Genesis 15 and 17 to be varying traditions of the same event told from different perspectives. On reading the final form of the narrative, however, we see the ups and downs of Abraham's journey of faith. In Genesis 17, God is once again the primary agent and the covenantal nature of the encounter is specified. Abraham is renamed in the process to represent this divine commitment. The eternal nature of the covenant is clarified and the promise of land is once again brought to bear. Distinctive in this episode is the sign of the covenant that God introduces.

Circumcision will henceforth mark God's covenant with Abraham and all that are his. Sarai, too, is renamed Sarah and the child from her womb is identified as Isaac. Thus, as the story progresses, the covenant develops further. Its sheer magnitude comes to the fore. When God finishes speaking, he departs. Abraham's agency as a participant is reduced; he simply receives the promise in silent awe. His ensuing action, however, is once again full obedience as he takes his entire house to be circumcised (vv. 23–27).

Abraham's agency is then reasserted in the following chapters, and his journey comes to its climax in Genesis 22. His winding path of growth and development over the last ten chapters of narrative has been building to this ultimate point of decision where "God puts Abraham to the test" and Abraham must confront not only his own true nature but also that of the God with whom he is covenanted. In this encounter, God, for the first time in their relationship, calls Abraham by name. In fact, Abraham is called three times by three different characters denoting the crucial nature of his role: first by God ("Abraham!" v. 1), then by Isaac ("my Father!" v. 7), and finally by the angel of God ("Abraham!" v. 11). Each time Abraham answers in the same fundamental manner. With this simple particle of existence, best translated as "Here I am," Abraham places himself directly before God in an unmediated way. This episode thus embodies a profound personal experience with God. The command to sacrifice his "only son," the beloved son of the promise, puts Abraham, who has been so obedient in action, to the ultimate test of faith. For his part, Abraham responds in word as well as deed, exemplifying that his faith in God's promise has finally matured with his obedience. By raising his hand to kill his son, Abraham's journey of faith reaches its goal and he is rewarded. Isaac is spared (as is Abraham) and a ram is given for the sacrifice. It is this sacrifice, the result of Abraham passing God's test, which ultimately seals his covenant of divine commitment with God. Abraham's story quickly comes to a close, his place in God's covenantal action in history assured. The remainder of Genesis details the fruition of God's promises as the descendants of Abraham become the Israelites, a great clan that eventually makes its way down into Egypt.

THE COVENANT THROUGH MOSES, THE SINAI COVENANT: EXODUS 19—24

From this point forward in the biblical narrative, there is a call and response necessary for the establishment of covenant with God. This covenant—both its promises and its obligations—expands as Israel grows from a family, the children of Israel, into a people. Exodus 19-24 provides the narrative of this step. Crucial to sealing this covenant is God's offer, "...if you obey my voice and keep my covenant, you shall be my treasured possession out of all the peoples" (19:5). And it is just an offer, not operative until the people accept. Several early OT books are dedicated to God giving his people all their obligations (Exod 20—31; Lev 1—27; Num 28—36; Deut 4—30). For their part, God's chosen people struggle with the covenant's demands, but this Law, the Torah in Hebrew, is given as the gift that guides the people into right relationship with God.

The Israelites, who had fallen into slavery, have struggled to make their exodus from Egypt under the leadership of Moses and now stand before God in the wilderness of the Sinai Peninsula (Exod 1—18). The solemn introduction to the Sinai covenant affirms that this covenant is different from those that God has established thus far. God uses Moses as a mediator to offer a conditional covenant to an entire people and has them respond first by word and then, only when the covenant is sealed, by deed. This is a development of the covenantal nature of God's relationship with the children of Israel. The divine commitment remains, but the human obligation in word and deed—in *relationship*—comes to the fore. The human component becomes operative: regardless of God's fidelity, the covenant can be broken. The people must "obey the voice" of God and "keep the covenant;" they must remain in active relationship with God and God alone. Abraham "hearkened to the voice" of another on occasion and caused his own stumbling on his journey, but his covenant was never at stake. In the conditional nature of this covenant, God presents its maintenance as dependent on this very obedience. Moses does as he is commanded, and the people respond positively in full voice, "Everything that the LORD has spoken we will do" (19:8). The people are then instructed to consecrate themselves for two days to prepare themselves, for "on the third day the LORD will come down upon Mount Sinai in the sight of all the people" (19:11). The appearance of God occurs on the third day, as promised (19:16–25).

The purpose of the consecration and appearance, or theophany, is so that God may initiate the covenant-making process through the giving of his words. Exodus 20 is devoted to the narration of these Ten Commandments, the Decalogue, in covenant form. God is identified as the covenant-giver, and, after a brief history of their relationship, the people are given the obligations of the covenant in the Ten Commandments. Witnessing to the theophany strikes fear in the people, leading them to ask Moses to be the official covenant mediator; thus formalizing his role as God's prophet. Moses agrees and urges the people not to fear but to understand the curses that are integral to the covenant relationship. He then draws near to God to receive further instruction, resulting in the laws that are often called the covenant collection or "book of the covenant." Exodus 20:22—23:19 begins and ends with legislation regarding ritual and the worship of God, so that all social interaction as the people of God is framed in worship. The last portion of this section recounts God's role in the covenant as military leader and protector of the people (23:20–33), grounded in the first commandment that God be their God alone.

Exodus 24 narrates the completion and ratification of the covenant in two rituals. Contingent upon the completion of the covenant seems to be the twofold reiteration of the people's commitment to exclusive relationship with God through keeping the covenant stipulations laid before them in the Ten Commandments. Here, for the first time in the biblical narrative, the human parties of a covenant with God make explicit their conscious commitment of *obedience* to God, rendering them full participants, active agents, in this covenantal relationship. Across the rest of Israel's Scriptures, this is the covenant that is operative. For this reason, Joshua calls the confederation of Israelite tribes to a covenant renewal ceremony at Shechem after the successful conquest of the promised land of Canaan (Josh 24). It is the demands of the Sinai covenant that determine the success or failure of both Israel as a whole and the lives of its individual people. Even after restoration from exile, it is this covenant that marks Ezra's reorganization and administration of the people (Neh 8—10). The characterization of God becomes more and more distant, but God's fidelity never wavers. The covenant abides.

THE COVENANT RENEWAL AT SHECHEM: JOSHUA 24

The Book of Joshua describes the conquest of Canaan, the land promised first to Abraham and then to the children of Israel at Sinai, in epic pageantry. In terms of a renewal of the Sinai covenant, the tribal assembly at Shechem narrated in Joshua 24 is of crucial importance to the creation of a unified people in a twelve-tribe league. By reaffirming the Sinai covenant, the people render themselves personal participants in that same covenant. Joshua 23 recounts the farewell speech of Joshua. Therefore, bringing the tribes together in covenant renewal to form a confederation is Joshua's final act as prophetic leader of the people of God. The final verses of Joshua 24, and the final verses of the book as a whole, recount Joshua's death and the faithfulness of Israel that he facilitated. When Joshua gathers "all the tribes of Israel to Shechem…before God" (v. 1) and initiates the address, "Thus says the LORD" (v. 2a), he places himself in the role of prophetic messenger and spokesman for God. When he recites the sacred history of Israel, he dwells on God's action on Israel's behalf in the exodus and the wilderness, but begins with the divine promises to the patriarchs. The purpose of the recitation for the current generation is found in the call to decision that follows.

Joshua 24:14–24 is marked, as are all the covenant-making passages, by imperative and response. The first commandment of Sinai is here reiterated in terms of service. God has already chosen Israel; it is now for Israel in the form of the tribal confederation to respond with their choice for God. And the people do so, three times. When they give their final response to the call, they affirm their determination to serve God by also vowing their obedience. It is only with the three-part response to God's offer of covenant, grounded in obedience, that the covenant renewal can be completed by way of a ceremonial ritual (24:25–28). The statutes and ordinances of the covenant made were written "in the book of the

Torah of God" and deposited in a sanctuary to God as witness to the covenant renewal. Joshua then dismisses the people to their tribal inheritances, made possible through their recommitment to the inherited covenant of their ancestors rendered alive and active in their own time.

THE COVENANT THROUGH DAVID: 2 SAMUEL 7

The story of David, the shepherd-turned-king of Israel, spans the Books of Samuel and continues into the first chapters of the Books of Kings. David enters the narrative of Israel's history at 1 Samuel 16 as a boy tending his father's flock in Bethlehem, but even at the first mention of his name, readers begin to understand the powerful role he will have in the national and religious developments to come: "Then Samuel took the horn of oil, and anointed him in the midst of his brothers; and the spirit of LORD came mightily upon David from that day forward" (1 Sam 16:13). David's rise to power is swift and direct from the moment he enters public life, first as a musician in King Saul's court, then as the king's armor-bearer and the champion who slays the Philistine Goliath. His special relationship with God is foreshadowed even in these early verses. By the time David becomes king (2 Sam 2), and certainly by the time of his death (2 Kgs 2), this relationship has become one of the most complex and intricately drawn in all of Israel's Scriptures. God's covenantal interaction with David takes the explicit form of a divine commitment, in terms of temple and dynasty, in 2 Samuel 7. The term *covenant* is not used explicitly here, but where this event is remembered in the Psalms, the term does characterize the nature of this divine promise (cf. Pss 89, 132). David's initiative to build a house for God is presented as providing the impetus for God to make this covenant. The theme of "dwelling" runs through this passage, such that the concepts of "house" and "dynasty" are interwoven to make up the divine promise. The chapter is divided broadly into two parts, with 7:1–17 comprising the divine promise and 7:18–29 making up David's prayerful response. All of 2 Samuel 7—8 provides a crux to the David story that underscores his personal relationship with God and his role as God's king and anointed one, or "messiah."

The divine promise of future glory and unmatched greatness is given through the prophet Nathan as a reaffirmation of a land for the people, in which they may live in peace and security. David's dynasty is assured by the establishment of an everlasting relationship. David is promised offspring who will build a house for God, and God likens their relationship to a father-son kinship of obedience and discipline as well as steadfast love and blessing. In his role as prophet, Nathan speaks "all these words" to David (v. 17). For his part, David enters the tent in which the ark of the covenant dwells, where he "sat before God" (v. 18). In a liturgical style, David extols the greatness and uniqueness of God who has made the divine presence known through his word, then recounts God's redeeming action on Israel's behalf through the exodus, when the people were set apart in God's name. With this prayer, David accepts God's covenantal promise, including the blessing and obedience that it entails. Through this covenant, God promises that a descendent of David will always be king over God's people. This king would be God's "anointed one," God's "messiah." Messianic expectations are now introduced as the hope of God's people whenever they find themselves suffering and oppressed by outsiders.

THE COVENANT TEXTS OF KNOWLEDGE AND TRUTH IN THE PROPHETS

Since our primary concern is to bring to light the covenantal background of the Fourth Evangelist's language and symbolism, an analysis of every covenantal text in each OT book in the Prophets is beyond our scope. The literary prophets do not make much use of the term *covenant* in their oracles, which could lead one to believe that the idea of covenant as the relationship between God and Israel was either unknown to the prophets (that is, not yet developed), or had been largely abandoned by them (that is, developed and discarded). Recent studies, however, have shown that the broad range of the concepts of "knowledge" and "truth" in ancient political relations serve to gauge the status of covenants and treaties. The prophets use this same imagery and language in the religious realm of Israel. The idea of "knowing God" reflects being in covenant with God, while the concept of "truth" signifies the origin and nature of this relationship as well as the fidelity inherent in maintaining it. Therefore, what follows are a few examples highlighting this covenantal language and imagery.

The prophet Hosea has long been associated with the use of covenant language and imagery. He is primarily remembered for using his own marriage as a metaphor for God's covenant with Israel, but his work is also teeming with imagery of knowledge and covenant obligation. Indeed, he makes a direct connection between knowledge of God and faithfulness to the Sinai covenant:

> Hear the word of the LORD, O people of Israel;
> for the LORD has an indictment against the inhabitants
> of the land.
> There is no faithfulness or loyalty,
> and no knowledge of God in the land.
> Swearing, lying, and murder,
> and stealing and adultery break out;
> bloodshed follows bloodshed.
> Therefore the land mourns,
> and all who live in it languish;
> together with the wild animals
> and the birds of the air,
> even the fish of the sea are perishing.
>
> (Hos 4:1–3)

Five of the Ten Commandments appear, and the "therefore" that connects them to the mourning, weakening, and perishing confirms the curses of the covenant breach. Knowledge of God is the required response to God's saving act and the resulting covenant bond. The lack of such knowledge leads to breaking this bond. Just what is it that God requires? Hosea clarifies God's role as well as God's demands on the people as he begins to conclude his work:

> I have been the LORD your God
> ever since the land of Egypt;
> you know no God but me,
> and besides me there is no savior.

13

It was I who fed you in the wilderness,
    in the land of drought.

(Hos 13:4–5)

The covenant bond is intimate and exclusive, and the people's ongoing knowledge of it and walking in it will continue to be their salvation.

The seventh- and sixth-century prophets, Jeremiah and Ezekiel, build upon this symbolism and covenantal understanding of knowledge. God's relationship with Israel is intimate, grounded in its Sinai role as God's chosen people and the obligatory response of absolute fidelity. In describing the hope for the future repentance of the people, Jeremiah reports,

> I will give them a heart to know that I am their LORD; and they shall be my people and I will be their God, for they shall return to me with their whole heart. (Jer 24:7)

Of course, Jeremiah's famous "new covenant" passage is probably the most telling—and the most beautiful—example of God's desire for the knowledge of the people in terms of their heart as well as their walk:

> The days are surely coming, says the LORD, when I will make a new covenant with the house of Israel and the house of Judah. It will not be like the covenant that I made with their ancestors when I took them by the hand to bring them out of the land of Egypt—a covenant that they broke, though I was their husband, says the LORD. But this is the covenant that I will make with the house of Israel after those days, says the LORD: I will put my law within them, and I will write it on their hearts; and I will be their God, and they shall be my people. No longer shall they teach one another, or say to each other, "Know the LORD," for they shall all know me, from the least of them to the greatest, says the LORD; for I will forgive their iniquity, and remember their sin no more. (Jer 31:31–34)

14

What is striking about this passage is not just the connection between knowing God and living in covenant with God, but the direct identification of the Sinai covenant with knowledge of God as well as the promise of a new covenant, built upon the old, which will be expressed and lived in a distinctive way. Like Jeremiah before him, Ezekiel believed the covenant that God will establish with his people in the future will have a distinctive character, yet be built solidly upon the old. This new covenant of peace will encompass both the action and the very being of those counted among God's sheep, yet will continue to be lived intimately in the knowledge of God.

The prophets employ the concept of "truth" to express the essential nature of this relationship. Through Jeremiah, God recounts the establishment of the covenant: "For I planted you as a choice vine, from the seed of truth" (2:21). Truth is also the language of living in covenant relationship with God. Through Zechariah, God commands the people,

> Render true judgments, show kindness and mercy to one another; do not oppress the widow, the orphan, the alien, or the poor; and do not devise evil in your hearts against one another. (Zech 7:9–10; see also 8:16–17)

Likewise, God commands the people to express their worship with the simple command: "Love truth and peace" (Zech 8:19).

The prophets also teach that the lack of truth is tantamount to a breach of covenant with God. Hosea uses both ideas to bring the covenant lawsuit against Israel:

> Hear the word of the LORD, O people of Israel;
> for the LORD has an indictment against the inhabitants
> of the land.
> There is no faithfulness or loyalty,
> and no knowledge of God in the land.
>
> (Hos 4:1)

The prophet Isaiah likewise describes life in Israel in breach of covenant as the failure of truth:

15

Justice is turned back,
>   and righteousness stands at a distance;
for truth stumbles in the public square,
>   and uprightness cannot enter.
Truth is lacking,
>   and whoever turns from evil is despoiled.

>   (Isa 59:14–15)

The failure, even death, of truth is also a fundamental component of Jeremiah's characterization of the breach of covenant. God has Jeremiah say to the people,

> This is the nation that did not obey the voice of the LORD their God, and did not accept discipline; truth has perished; it is cut off from their lips. (Jer 7:28)

Finally, the prophets also incorporate the language of truth into their message of restoration and covenant renewal that will follow the people's repentance and recommitment to God. The prophet Isaiah characterizes the repentant remnant of Israel as restoring its covenant relationship to God in truth:

> On that day the remnant of Israel and the survivors of the house of Jacob will no more lean on the one who struck them, but will lean on the LORD, the Holy One of Israel, in truth. (Isa 10:20)

Isaiah further summarizes both the character of God and the character of the new covenant with the restored Israel in this concept of faithfulness and truth. This is the blessing of living with God in covenant love, knowledge, and fidelity:

> Then whoever invokes a blessing in the land
>   shall bless by the God of faithfulness,
> and whoever takes an oath in the land
>   shall swear by the God of truth;
> because the former troubles are forgotten
>   and are hidden from my sight.

>   (Isa 65:16)

THE COVENANT RENEWAL AT JERUSALEM: NEHEMIAH 8—10

The holy city of Jerusalem was overrun by the Babylonians in 587 BC. The temple was destroyed and the people of Judah were exiled across the Babylonian Empire. The Books of Ezra and Nehemiah recount the end of the exile and the return and restoration of the land following the Edict of Cyrus, king of Persia, in 538 BC. After much conflict and struggle, the people of Judah rebuilt their temple in 515 BC. Nehemiah 8 records that Ezra read a book of the Law in the hearing of all Jerusalem. This could be the first reading of the Torah as we now have it. Further, Nehemiah 10 recounts that Ezra organized a formal ratification of the covenant of Moses after the feast of Tabernacles. Later Jewish tradition considers Ezra a second Moses, attributing the definitive editing of the Torah to him. These chapters therefore warrant a brief look as they provide the most contemporaneous covenant tradition to John's own time and place.

The restoration of the exiled people of Judah to their land culminates in the momentous event of rededication to Torah, thus paralleling the covenant-making events in the wilderness at Sinai with regard to the formation of the people of God. All the people gather and their initiative is the impetus behind the reading and renewal. The narrative is careful to assert the people's full understanding of the Torah they heard, as well as their verbal assent to the blessing of God. The Torah is then implemented in the celebration of the festival of tabernacles as prescribed. The covenant renewal itself is presented in terms of confession and commitment. The people acknowledge the steadfast love of God as the integral component of his covenant-keeping in their final plea for continued protection in relationship. They close in prayer and confirm their commitment to God in writing. The communal pledge of commitment reflects the stipulations of covenantal behavior that the people take upon themselves.

Two notable points arise from this account of covenant renewal after the Exile. First, although covenant-making practices resonate throughout the narrative, including public reading, recitation of the historical relationship between God and his people, promises, obligations, and witness to the seal of the covenant, on the whole this covenant renewal does not follow a form we have seen before in the biblical narrative. The second point is correlative to the first: In this case, the entire impetus for renewal is the motivation of the people. God is not an active agent in this account. We have come to the opposite extreme from the covenant with Noah, where he was the silent responder to God's directive for action. Here the people of Israel take on the full role of renewal instigator, bearing all the consequences of their decision and actions. They do all the talking. As a people they have long ago been "chosen," God's presence is a given, and God's covenant-making and covenant-keeping character of love and loyalty in relationship is well known. What has been missing through the exile is the people's obedient response in action to the covenantal promises of Torah—a situation that is remedied in Nehemiah 8—10.

Characteristics of the Covenant Relationship

Five fundamental characteristics can be articulated from the covenantal narrative preserved in the OT. The first and most basic characteristic is the aspect of *chosenness*. In the narratives of God's covenantal interaction with humankind, God is always the primary agent: God determines to make the covenant and God chooses those through whom he will implement his plan for creation. The second characteristic of the OT covenant relationship is the offer of *covenantal promises*. Those chosen by God to participate in covenant relationship are made promises in establishing that bond. In the earlier covenants with Adam, Noah, and Abraham, God's promises are straightforward and direct. Yet, when the promises are conditional and couched in terms of blessing or punishment as with the Sinai covenant through Moses, the primary benefit to the human participants is the promise of becoming, remaining, or renewing their role as God's "chosen people" or "treasured possession." The covenant seals the promise and accepts these mutual roles. The third characteristic is the corollary human response to the first two characteristics: *covenantal obedience in action*. In the narratives of Noah and Abraham, it

18

is not necessary for the chosen recipients of God's covenantal promises to speak to God in any way; they simply act in accordance with God's imperative. Beginning with Abraham, however, the human response becomes more complex as the human relationship with God develops. The response shifts from the physical alone to both the physical and the spiritual, as indicated by verbal interaction with God. Humankind's disposition before God and in relationship with God becomes more significant as the world it inhabits becomes more complex. By the end of the OT covenant history, the human response effectively takes over the lead role in the covenant narrative from God's initiating activity. However, in every stage of this narrative, the fundamental quality of the response remains the same: obedience. Full, unmediated obedience to God's imperative, be it physical or a complex integration of the physical and the spiritual/verbal, is demanded both to establish and to renew covenantal relationship with God.

The first three characteristics of the OT covenant relationship each build upon the other to establish the relationship itself. This relationship makes possible the fourth characteristic: *the abiding presence of God* in creation and in the midst of human life. The Sinai covenant demanded the construction of the tabernacle as the dwelling place for God in the people's midst. This *shekinah* or "dwelling presence" of God in the midst of his covenanted people becomes of primary concern from this point forward, and, in the days of Solomon, results in the construction of the temple that becomes the focus of Israelite worship. Furthermore, the motivation behind the covenant renewal ceremonies in the days of Joshua and Ezra is to ensure this presence of God.

Articulating the fifth and final characteristic of the OT covenant relationship in many ways brings us to the purpose of the entire overview: *knowledge* in terms of *making God known*. The covenant promises establish the manner by which God knows his chosen people and the manner by which they may know God. This knowledge includes understanding God's binding loyalty (in terms of *steadfast love*) and faithfulness (in terms of *truth*) in kinship with his people. The flourishing of this knowledge of God made possible through the dynamic of daily living in covenantal obedience breathes life into the relationship between God and his people. Likewise, the failure of this knowledge threatens the very existence of the covenantal relationship, and thereby the existence of the people of God. To live in the truth of the love and knowledge of God is the fundamental purpose and the overarching hope of the OT covenant relationship.

The themes gleaned from a narrative review of the OT covenant texts provide the language used to articulate covenantal hope and its resulting lived experience in the Gospel story. The language of knowledge, love, truth, and familial kinship in the context of Israel's Scripture is thus the language of covenant. The OT covenantal texts and the celebrations that recall God's covenantal saving action in the past and render that action present in the current community provide the symbolism for ongoing use of the covenant metaphor. It is from this rich storehouse that the Fourth Evangelist drew for his expression of Jesus as the revelation of God's new covenant activity in creation on behalf of humankind, the children of God.

Questions for Review

1. What are the major covenantal stories of the OT narrative? Who are the mediators of this developing covenantal relationship, and how might they come into play in the Gospel story of the new covenant?
2. Given the developing covenantal relationship narrated in the OT, how might covenant be the primary means through which God relates to humankind?
3. What are the primary characteristics of the covenant relationship presented in Israel's Scripture? Suggest how the Evangelist might interweave these characteristics through his Gospel account without directly using the term.

2

JOHN AND SCRIPTURE

Beginnings of the Word

Closer examination of the narrative of the Gospel of John entails an initial exploration of its underlying structure. Interpreters study the final composition of a biblical author and try to glean what the original outline would have been if the author wrote one. This is done in order to get a sense of the author's flow of thought which, in turn, aids in exegeting, or drawing out his intention in writing. Because we do this after the fact and we cannot ask the author about his structuring techniques, we can never be certain about this process. Nonetheless, the almost universal approach to structuring the Fourth Gospel notes four major components. A Prologue (1:1–18) is followed by the body of the narrative which is presented in two parts: Jesus' public ministry, commonly called the Book of Signs (1:19–12:50), and his departure, including a last discourse, the passion, and postresurrection appearances, often called the Book of Glory (13:1—20:31). The conclusion to the body of the Gospel is followed by an epilogue (21:1–25).

In order to arrive at this road map for entering the narrative world of the Fourth Gospel, we look for textual markers that serve as signposts along the way. The poetic Prologue (1:1–18) provides the words of an insider—the all-knowing narrator who communicates to the readers everything they need to know to begin the Gospel. John 1:19 shifts to prose and begins the story itself with Jesus moving about with disciples and teaching in public throughout Galilee and Judea. Along the way, Jesus refers to his "hour" that is coming and will change the world as they know it.

This "hour" finally arrives at verse 12:23 and Jesus signals the end of his public ministry. A new period of private ministry to Jesus' disciples thus begins at verse 13:1 and flows through his arrest, death, and resurrection to verse 20:29, with the final verses (20:30–31) serving as a conclusion to the body of the Gospel—a first ending. Then we read John 21, an afterword to this story that looks to the future of the community formed by the narrative. The structure of the Gospel of John can therefore be diagrammed as follows:

1:1–18 The Prologue
　Introduction to the Nature and Mission of the Word
1:19—12:50 The Book of Signs
　The Word Reveals Himself to the World and through a
　　Public Ministry
1:19–1:51 The First Days of Gradual Revelation of Jesus
　The Calling of the First Disciples
2:1—4:54 The Journey from Cana to Cana
　The Educational Journey of Faith
5:1—10:42 The Feasts of Judaism
　The Perfection of Old Testament Feasts and the Theme of
　　Life
11:1—12:50 The Movement to Death and Glory
　The Arrival of the Hour of Jesus and the Culmination of
　　Life and Light
13:1—20:31 The Book of Glory
　The Word Makes God Known and Is Glorified in Death and
　　Resurrection
13:1—17:26 The Last Discourse
　The Foot Washing and the Prediction of Betrayal and
　　Denial
　The Last Discourse with the Disciples
18:1—19:42 Jesus' Passion and Death
　The Arrest, Trial, Crucifixion, Death, and Burial of Jesus
20:1–31 The Resurrection and Encounters with the Disciples
21:1–25 The Epilogue
　Concluding Resurrection Appearance in Galilee of
　　Theological and Communal Importance

The Prologue (John 1:1–18)

In her work on the NT narratives, biblical scholar Morna Hooker notes that there is often a literary and thematic connection between the beginning and ending of a composition. Strong endings often take us back to where we began, and skillful storytelling techniques often remind us that it was the writer's purpose all along to lead us to precisely this point.[1] In the rest of this chapter, we will focus on the beginning of the Gospel of John as the gateway into both the story itself and the good news the Evangelist is teaching through this story. The spotlight will rest upon the Prologue (1:1–18), we can then reflect upon how this beginning prepares us for the story to come.

The term *prologue* comes to us from the Greek word *logos*, which means "word" but has larger connotations of "speech" or "study," and the prefix *pro*, meaning "before." The term *logos* becomes an important concept in the content of the Prologue, but initially it also helps us to understand that the first eighteen verses of the Gospel of John serve as a message before the body of the narrative. As we see in some contemporary novels, the prologue serves as an introduction, giving background that sets up the action and helps readers make sense of the story to come. Further, this becomes information that readers have that most characters in the story *don't* have. Readers are thus put in a privileged position as we participate in the action of the story, identifying with this or that character and waiting, even hoping, for them to catch on, as it were, and begin to grasp the fullness of what is at stake. In ancient Greek tragedy, the prologue was the first component of the play that set forth the subject and protagonists of the drama when the chorus entered the stage. The prologue would typically give the mythological background necessary for understanding the events of the play. By "mythological," we refer to the interaction of the divine with the earthly, and in the case of the Gospel of John, to how God interacts with God's creation. The Prologue

---

1. Morna Hooker, *Endings: Invitations to Discipleship* (Peabody, MA: Hendrickson, 2003), 3. See also Morna Hooker, *Beginnings: Keys That Open the Gospels* (Harrisburg, PA: Trinity Press International, 1997). For detail of the Johannine Prologue as the key to interpreting the Gospel, see 64–83.

therefore introduces the setting, previews the main characters, and establishes the primary themes for the work. Although we as readers may not fully understand the enigmatic philosophical ideas and motifs of the Prologue, they create the tension that begs the question of the *how* of God's action in the world. The subsequent narrative *shows* what the Prologue *tells*. John 1:1–18 is therefore a carefully composed prologue that is essential to understanding the rest of the narrative.

The next step in interpreting what the Evangelist is teaching in this "first page" of the Gospel is to explore how he has organized it. By writing a Gospel, the Fourth Evangelist is sharing good news and teaching that God has broken into history with a new act of covenant. God is faithful and yet has done something distinctive through this new covenant. The use of the poetic Prologue as a foundation for his Gospel that suddenly and definitively breaks into prose narrative can be understood as a reflection of this theological perspective. The incarnation of the Word of God suddenly and definitively turns the custom and "truth" of the world on its ear, for this is the story of God's self-revelation in history. The complexity of these eighteen verses, however, should not deter us from experiencing their beauty or taking in the Evangelist's core proclamations. To aid in this endeavor, R. Alan Culpepper suggests that the Evangelist begins with cosmic assertions of the eternal nature of God and God's Word and moves to more specific claims of the interaction of the Word of God in creation in terms of a familial relationship. The crux of the Prologue seems to be that Jesus gives those who believe in him "power to become children of God" (v. 12). John is then able to proclaim the incarnation of the Word in Jesus Christ as God's promised gift of truth to humankind who, in turn, reveals God to all who receive him.[2] Since beginnings are the manners by which our Evangelist presents the key to understanding all that follows, Culpepper's road map will serve as the guide through which we can examine the key with which the Fourth Evangelist provides us to navigate his Gospel. If verse 12b is indeed the central thesis of the Prologue, this proclamation also

2. R. Alan Culpepper, "The Pivot of John's Prologue," *New Testament Studies* 27 (1980): 1–31.

indicates the aim of the entire mission of both Christ and the narrative that shares this good news.

IN THE BEGINNING WAS THE WORD OF GOD (vv. 1–11)

The first words of the Prologue, and thus of the entire Gospel, are identical with the opening words of Genesis: "In the beginning." They serve to bring the Fourth Evangelist's first audience to "the beginning," not only of this narrative but to the beginnings of its sacred narrative of history, when God spoke creation into existence (Genesis 1—3). By echoing this shared story of God's action in history, the Evangelist firmly grounds his story to come in the world of the Sacred Scripture of Israel. This literary intention is developed with the fullness of the phrase: "In the beginning was the Word." The Evangelist's choice of "the Word" (*logos* in Greek) allows for rich and varied symbolism, evoking God's revelation in Torah as well as the broader voice of the sages through the Greco-Roman cultural milieu. "The Word" that is introduced here corresponds with God's own word of creation in the beginning, now described as a being who is divine, eternal, and in relationship with God (v. 2). In a poetic fashion, the Evangelist teaches that as an independent being of the same divine essence as God, the Word is fundamentally oriented toward union with God. The expansiveness of this first verse prepares readers for God's revelatory action in the story to come.

The following verses present the nature and role of the *logos* as the vehicle for creation who is the giver of life and stands fast in the darkness, lighting the way for humankind (vv. 3–5). The Word's role in all creation is foundational for understanding him as the giver of "life" and "light." The Evangelist introduces these themes of life, light, and its corresponding darkness that will play out across the rest of the narrative, but also continues an exposition of Genesis 1 that echoes the eternal creative force of God. The final words of verse 5 further hint at the conflict to come between the Word as giver of light (Gen 1:3–5) and the darkness that exists among the people who are the caretakers of God's creation (Gen 1:26–30). A physical threat to this newly characterized Word is implicated as well as the notion of the Word already in the world, in the form of

Torah, which has not been fully understood. Nonetheless, in regard to the shining light, the darkness "did not overcome it."

The first human being is now introduced into the story, a man named John (vv. 6–8). We should clarify here that, although the Evangelist never calls him "the Baptist," this John is the same person that the other Gospels call "John the Baptist" (and not John the Evangelist). In the Prologue, this human being is characterized as having come to be, in distinction from the eternally existing Word. In the same breath, however, the Evangelist describes this man as "sent from God," the only fully human character in the narrative to be identified as such. John, then, is special: he is sent into the world from God with a mission. This man can be trusted. His mission is to testify; to bear witness to the light of the eternal Word (vv. 7–8). Through the introduction of John and his role, the Evangelist also introduces the concept of belief in the Word. Scholars often notice that *belief* as a noun (*pistis*) does not occur in the Fourth Gospel, but forms of the verb *to believe* (*pisteuō* / *pisteuomai*) occur regularly and often (ninety-eight times). Thus, faith in the Gospel of John is always dynamic and active and is rightly described in terms of a process, or better, a journey. John, the human witness, is crucial to point to the light and facilitate the journey of faith.

The next segment of the Prologue flows out of the final words of verses 6–8 and returns focus to the light, now further characterized as "truth" (vv. 9–10). The true light whose enlightening reign reaches everyone is coming into the world. The incarnation foreshadowed here comes to pass in the counterpart to these verses, verse 14. The imminent conflict of the Gospel story is also reaffirmed, this time in terms of "knowledge" (v. 10; see v. 8). The very world of which the light was instrumental in creating did not know him. Aspects of the language and symbolism of covenant (truth, knowledge, and Torah) are brought further into the Prologue's presentation of the person and mission of the Word. Verse 11 then provides powerful parallelism to this disconnect between the light and the world through the intimate language of "his own." The Word, instrumental giver of life and light in intimate relationship with God, comes into what is his own and is not received by his own people. Giving, receiving, and rejecting in relationship thus become the operative interactivity of the incarnation of the Word.

THE HEART OF THE PROLOGUE: BECOMING CHILDREN OF GOD (V. 12)

We now arrive at the heart of the Prologue. Put another way, the force of the entire Prologue is poised on the fulcrum of the mission of the Word to give "power to become children of God" (v. 12b). The mission of the Word that has become human in Jesus the Christ is to give the gift of truth that empowers those who receive and believe in him to become children of God. Notice that I identified the heart of the Prologue as "verse 12b." When a verse is made up of several clauses in the same sentence or even several sentences and we want to focus on just part of the verse, the convention is to mark each phrase with a letter of the alphabet beginning with the letter *a*. In this case, John 1:12 can be divided into three phrases, verses 12a, 12b, and 12c. In the original Greek text of the Gospel, a direct translation of the full verse would be: "But to those who did receive him, he gave power to become children of God, to those who believe in his name." Verse 12b is the central phrase of the verse and the central concept of the Prologue. In an attempt to make the sentence more understandable, not all English translations preserve this original word order. This is an acceptable practice. Therefore we must highlight the Evangelist's word order in order to highlight the central meaning.

This core proclamation, the giving to those who receive the Word the power to become children of God, is the heart of the Prologue's message. Therefore, this core must also profoundly affect the remainder of the Prologue. The establishment of childhood to God through the Son of God is the culmination of all God's dealings with the world, the goal of the Creator and creation. The claim is that those who receive the Word will be given the power to become children of God, but how does one go about receiving him in order to achieve this status? By believing in his name (v. 12c). The remainder of the Prologue thus sheds light on how we receive and believe in the Word, what it means to become "children of God," and how this could be the goal of the whole Gospel.

GIFT UPON GIFT: THE WORD BECAME FLESH AND DWELT AMONG US (vv. 13–18)

Those who believed, received the Word and thereby received a gift, the power to become children of God. Verse 13 supplements the description of the role of the "receivers" in this relationship by characterizing the role of God and the "how" of becoming God's children. The husband's will, ordinary human sexual desire, and ethnic descent do no avail, for spiritual birth comes from above, from heaven. This notion is more fully articulated in the discourse of John 3 but is introduced here in terms of the mission of the Word. Because of the coming of the Word into the world and the rejection by "his own," heritage and race are rendered irrelevant to birth from God and the privilege of becoming the covenant people of God also changes forever. The Sinai covenant will be fulfilled and a new covenant put in place.

The Evangelist now returns to what God did to make this possible. Verses 9–10 reveal that the Word, characterized as "the true light," was "coming into the world." Corresponding to this proclamation, verse 14 majestically announces how this happened, who the Word becomes, and what he gives in the process:

> And the Word became flesh and pitched his tent among us, and we beheld his glory, the glory as of a father's only son, full of the gift which is truth.

These words are powerful indeed, and their impact should not be minimized. They announce an event, long coming in the flow of the Prologue, and made possible by the plan of God to re-envision the covenant people as children of spiritual, not human, birth. I have offered my own, more literal translation to highlight the Evangelist's careful word choice. Just as God's action in the Sinai covenant and the giving of the Torah changed the nature of God's relationship with creation, the incarnation of the Word, while very much in accord with that history, once again decisively alters the manner by which creation can relate to God. The Evangelist leaves no doubt as to the full humanity of the incarnate Word with the use of *flesh* to describe this in-breaking of God's action. Further, the exodus event and the covenant-making time in the wilderness at Sinai are brought to mind with the action of dwelling "among us." The verb *skēnoō* means literally to "pitch a tent" and the form here is generally translated as "lived" or "made his dwelling." The Evangelist's verb choice, however, resonates with Exodus 33—40, where God renews the covenant with Israel mediated by Moses, and the people are told to make a tent (the tabernacle, the *skēnē*,) so that God can live among them. After a lengthy description of the tabernacle and its construction, Exodus 40 recounts the erection of the tabernacle and the placement of the tablets of the Torah in the ark of the covenant and its setting in the holy of holies. Depicting the incarnation of the Word in terms of the *shekinah*, or dwelling presence of God, thus also preserves the Word's divinity as a new presence of God and God's covenantal activity in creation. This echo would not have been lost on the Evangelist's first audience.

The incarnate Word made his dwelling "among us." The narration shifts to the first person plural as the narrator speaks inclusively from the perspective of the children of God. This inclusive narration also draws the audience into the potentiality of becoming part of this group. "We have seen his glory." The visible and powerful manifestation of God likewise recalls the revelation of the glory of God to Moses on Mount Sinai (Exodus 19—24; 33—34), but now this revelation is described as a father's only son. This phrase introduces the Evangelist's characteristic christological formulation: Jesus is the Son of God. The verse also offers a very human image of the incomparably privileged status of Jesus as "the only son" of God as Father, ensuring that Jesus' status in relation to God is understood to be unique. This powerful statement concludes by further describing the incarnate Word to be full of "grace" and "truth." Many interpreters simply understand this phrase as descriptive and take the juxtaposition of "grace" and "truth" as expressing the OT covenant love of God, reflecting the common OT pairing of covenant love and truth (see, for example, Exod 34:6). This reading has much to commend it, but we must note the Evangelist's use of the Greek word *charis* (usually translated as "grace") instead of the word for "love." Thus, without dismissing a reflection of pure covenant love, a more complete interpretation may be Francis J. Moloney's observation that by translating the Greek word *charis* with its more widely held denotation of "an expression of good will, a gift, an unexpected favor," and reading the "and" as explanatory, thus allowing the second term, "truth," to clarify the first term, the phrase is rendered more clearly as "full of a gift which is truth."[3] The Word, giver of light and life, now incarnate, is filled with a new gift, truth. The giving and receiving of this gift of truth is intimately connected to the power to become children of God and, thus, to the crux of the mission of the incarnate Word. In OT terms, this gift of truth would also entail the unified relationship with God that is produced by covenantal obedience. The remainder of the Prologue returns to where it began by continuing to elucidate this gift, integrating it into the life and being of the Word now made human.

The incarnate Word is then firmly grounded in history as the narrator returns to John the Baptist, the human witness sent by God whose testimony readers can trust (v. 15). John provides the first direct speech of the Gospel. John himself repeats the narrator's major verbs about him thus far, thereby confirming in direct speech what the narrator claimed for him. He testifies that the Word is "the one who comes" after him temporally, but ranks before him. With this historical grounding and temporal designation in place, the Prologue surges forward with the mission of the Word. The narrator again speaks in the collective voice of the children of God to detail the process of God's action in creation in terms of their reception of God's gifts (v. 16). Retaining the earlier understanding of *charis* as "gift," what God has done through the incarnate Word is to give the gift (of truth) upon a gift. The nature of the new gift was introduced in verse 14 and the nature of the first gift has been behind the very characterization of the Word in verses 1–5, but both are illuminated in verse 17:

---

3. Francis J. Moloney, *The Gospel of John*, Sacra Pagina 4 (Collegeville, MN: Liturgical Press, 1998), 39–45.

The law indeed was given through Moses; the gift of
truth came to be through Jesus Christ.

The law was a gift from God, and the reference to Moses
ensures that the covenantal gift of Torah echoes through this
proclamation. The gift of truth was given through the incarnation
of the Word, who is finally identified in history as Jesus, who is
the Christ (from the Greek word for "Messiah"). This gift of truth
is likewise a gift of God that acts in history in covenant with creation. But one cannot "replace" the other. Rather, the gift of the
Law is perfected in the gift of the incarnation. The giving of the
gift of the Torah was God's covenantal activity at Sinai. The incarnation of the Word that is full of the gift of truth is God's
covenantal activity in Jesus.

The final verse of the Prologue returns to the beginning (vv.
1–2) while illuminating the relationship of Jesus as "the only
son" to the Father who is turned toward that Father, now in history (v. 18). It is the Son who makes God known, and in this way
gives humankind the ability to become children of God. This is
indeed a new covenantal move in history. Jesus, the Word of God
made human, will make God known through his life and ministry. The remainder of the Gospel will narrate the "how" of the
covenantal claim that the Prologue introduces. In essence, the
new covenant gives the power to become children of God through
receiving the gift of truth as revealed by Jesus Christ the only Son,
who is in perfect relationship with God the Father.

Beginnings of the Covenant of the
Children of God

John 1:1–18 is one of the most famous texts of the NT. It is
poetic and beautiful, even while it is enigmatic and provocative.
As a prologue, it sets the stage for all that is to come, introducing
key characters (God, Jesus the Christ and Word of God, John the
Baptist, the world, and Jesus' own people the Jews) and key
themes (word, light, dark, life, family, truth, covenant, knowledge, and the revelation of God) of the Gospel. As such it is indis-

pensable information for readers as we launch into the body of the narrative. The structure of the Prologue further points us toward the mission of the Word made human in this world and the hope of the new covenantal activity of God in truth: that everyone who encounters the Word may receive and believe in him, thus becoming the new children of God in the family formed by Jesus, the Christ and Son of God. Therefore this new covenant gift of truth is available to anyone and everyone, regardless of race and ethnicity. All humankind has to do is receive him and believe in his Word.

Questions for Review

1. Why is so much attention given to the Prologue of the Gospel of John? How does its structure help in understanding it? What is its purpose in the flow of the Gospel narrative?
2. What key terms, themes, and characters are introduced in the Prologue? How do they begin to play out in the rest of John 1?
3. Which of these terms and themes introduced in the Prologue are also the language and symbolism of covenant?
4. How does it affect your reading of the Gospel to begin by thinking of Jesus as the Gift of Truth and potential believers as the children of God?

3

THE PUBLIC MINISTRY
OF JESUS

Covenant in the Book of Signs

We now find ourselves at John 1:19 and the beginning of the body of the narrative of the Gospel according to John. After the Prologue, there is a continuous narrative from John 1:19—12:50 through which Jesus emerges and conducts his public ministry. This first part of the story narrates the public ministry of Jesus of Nazareth and is often called the Book of Signs. The final two paragraphs of John 12 offer a summary description and analysis of Jesus' public ministry and its effect (vv. 37–43) followed by the last words of Jesus in public directed to the people in general (vv. 44–50). John 13:1–3 marks a shift in emphasis, and all of Jesus' teachings in John 13—17 are directed to "his own"—the new children of God that Jesus has gathered across his public ministry described in the Prologue. The spirit of these divisions was introduced in verses 11–13 of the Prologue. Jesus came into his own people who did not receive him, but for all those who do, during his earthly ministry and beyond, Jesus continues to teach and give the gift of truth as members of the new family of God. The second part of the story therefore narrates the consequences of the public ministry and the glorification of Jesus the Christ, and is thus often called the Book of Glory. The covenantal components of the first part of John's particular account of the good news will be discussed in this chapter and the second part in the next.

Introduction to the Book of Signs

John 1:19—12:50 is often designated the Book of Signs because these chapters largely concern Jesus' miracles, what this Evangelist always refers to as "signs," and the discourses that interpret those signs. This Evangelist chooses seven representative signs of the many Jesus performed in order to *signify* the wondrous power of God through Jesus—much like that of God through Moses during the covenantal period in the Sinai wilderness recounted in Exodus. They are:

2:1–12 The Turning of Water to Wine at the Wedding Feast at Cana
4:45–54 The Healing of the Royal Official's Child at Cana
5:1–12 The Healing of the Crippled Man
6:1–15 The Feeding of the Multitude
6:16–21 The Walking on Water
9:1–41 The Healing of the Man Born Blind
11:1–44 The Raising of Lazarus at Bethany

The placement of these signs, however, does not determine the overall flow of the Book of Signs. In fact, we will see that if the people Jesus encounters understand the signs as ends or goals in themselves, Jesus will push them further to believe in his word as the revelation of the new covenant in God. Deeds, however miraculous, will not sustain faith. Jesus calls people into a deeper, and more challenging, relationship. This seems to be true for the Evangelist's storytelling structure as well. The Book of Signs flows in four parts from the early days of the revelation (1:19–51), through a journey that teaches about faith (2:1—4:54), into the heart of the ministry and the feasts of Judaism (5:1—10:42), onto a final movement toward glory (11:1—12:50). Through this pattern of the Evangelist's storytelling cloth, we can discuss the covenantal fabric of the Book of Signs.

Early Days of the Revelation of Jesus (1:19–51)

The Prologue of John's Gospel presents Jesus Christ as the incarnate Word who fulfills the Torah of the Sinai covenant and gives a new covenant, the gift of truth, to those who would be children of God (1:1–18). The bridge from the Prologue to the action of the body of the Gospel is manifested in the human witness sent from God named John. He becomes the embodiment of the Prologue as he continues to give valuable information about the person of Jesus as well as about the story to come, now in the form of dialogues with other human characters. The Prologue tells the reader the *who* and the *what* of the events at hand, but leaves open the *how*. The story itself is necessary to understand how it all happens. John the Baptist, introduced so strongly in the Prologue as the human witness sent from God, then opens the narrative as the first character in the story with dialogical force. In other words, he is the first human character to speak, and in his first dialogue, he takes control and begins to teach the *how* of the good news. As readers often notice, John is not referred to as "the Baptist" in this Gospel, as his role in this narrative is as a "witness" who testifies to God's action in and through Jesus. He is the one character who witnesses accurately to the Word made flesh, just as he was sent to do. His first dialogue at 1:19–28, followed by the monologue of 1:29–34, and his final initial witness in 1:35–42, provide readers the grounds from which to form decisions about the characters in the narrative, and about their own belief in the Word. Jesus and his gathering disciples are introduced during the Baptist's teaching and can then take over the dialogue for the final verses of the chapter (1:43–51).

The movement of the beginning of the body of John's Gospel (1:19–51) is marked temporally across the span of the first week of Jesus' ministry (vv. 29, 35, 43; then 2:1). Thus, 1:19–28 narrates day one, 1:29–34 narrates day two, 1:35–42 narrates day three, 1:43–51 narrates day four, followed by a distinctive three-day gap before the narration picks up again (2:1). This structuring of time is often seen as a week of new creation, and this could well be part of the Evangelist's plan, especially with the imagery from the Book of Genesis we have seen across both the Prologue

35

and these first days. However, we should also note that a primary motif of these early verses that remains in play throughout this Gospel is *revelation*. If a cue is taken from Exodus 19:15–16 ("on the third day…"), then the first four days plus the three-day narrative gap do not only point to creation but also refer to the revelation of God on Mt. Sinai that results in God's covenant with Israel. The *Mekilta on Exodus* is a work from later Jewish rabbis that presents explicit instructions on how the people are to spend four days preparing prior to the three actual days of preparation for the ancient celebration of Pentecost, the commemoration of the gift of the Law on Sinai. The first three days show John the Baptist living out everything claimed about him in the Prologue; he thus accurately portrays his own role on day one and points to Jesus as the Lamb of God on day two. In days three and four, the gathering disciples begin to heap titles onto Jesus: *Rabbi, Messiah, Son of God, King of Israel*. But separately none of these titles go far enough—they remain in the religious and political categories within which the disciples are comfortable. Jesus constantly shatters comfortable categories and challenges those he encounters into deeper relationship with him. Thus, at the end of day four, Jesus rebuffs Nathanael and prepares them all for the revelatory process to come in terms of his own role as the Son of Man who reveals God's glory (v. 51).

John 1 teaches its readers much about God and how God is working in the world. The Prologue affirms that God is Creator and the activity recounted in the Gospel to come is grounded in God's creative, covenantal activity of Genesis 1. Further, this story has to be understood in terms of God's covenantal activity at Sinai recounted in Exodus. That covenant was a gift of God through Moses; this new covenant is a further gift given by God, a gift of truth, made possible by the incarnation of God's Son, Jesus Christ. The role of this Word of God in human form is to communicate, to reveal and make God known to all who will listen. The tension sparked by the word of Jesus creates dramatic interactions through dialogue. Jesus begins this process here and carries it across his story, actively moving it to its fulfillment on the cross that glorifies both God and the Son and produces a new covenantal community of God's children who have received the

Word. Jesus is the Lamb of God who heals the broken, sinful relationship between God and humankind, and the Son of Man who reveals God in the human story by challenging disciples and readers to "come and see."

The Journey of Faith from Cana to Cana (2—4)

In John 2—4, the audience of the Gospel participates in Jesus' travel from Cana in Galilee, south into Jerusalem and the environs of Judea, returning north through Samaria, and finally back up into Galilee and Cana, but also has the discipleship-oriented episodes of 1:19–51 at the forefront of consciousness. At the close of those first days, the disciples seem to be coming to an authentic faith and understanding of Jesus and the Christology of the Gospel. But then Jesus challenges Nathanael. This is part of the teaching strategy of the Gospel: whenever people seem to come to a solid articulation of faith, Jesus engages them in dialogue and challenges them to go further. But if the disciples need to go further, where must they go? The Evangelist answers this question across the narrative journey from Cana to Cana.

This portion of Jesus' public ministry—what we'll call the Cana to Cana narrative—provides the Johannine instruction on the nature of authentic faith. The two signs at Cana in Galilee that form the beginning and ending of this teaching are the literary frames of the journey of faith. The physical movement between these two events mirrors the theological journey through which Jesus brings himself and his word of God to potential receivers and believers across the world, first in a Jewish setting then in a larger, non-Jewish setting. This portion of the Gospel thus offers the universal possibility of a journey of faith. For this Evangelist, faith is dynamic and communicative, and whenever Jesus' dialogue partners think they "have it" and "have arrived," Jesus verbally challenges them to go further. We also begin to see a constant tension in the expectation and acceptance of "signs-faith." The revelation of God in Jesus must always be anchored in the relationship he offers as well as in the message of his life, death, and glorification, not in the fleeting "wow" of a miraculous experience. Jesus encounters these different people or groups of people and challenges them to move out of their comfort zones and religious preconceptions and move into a new covenant relationship with God the Father through himself, Jesus the Son. We see examples of types of responses to this challenge both from within Judaism and from the broader non-Jewish, or Gentile, world. Each encounter provides a model for a faith response, some positive, some negative, and some, like Nicodemus, try to ride the fence between both worlds. Although this may be acceptable for the meantime, Jesus will ultimately push all those he encounters to make a firm decision of faith.

The first days of Jesus' public life were focused on the testimony of John the Baptist and the gathering of the first disciples (1:19–51). The entire ministry of John the Baptist had pointed to Jesus as the Word of God set forth in the Prologue (1:1–2, 19–37). The gathering disciples, however, have much to learn. Regardless of their earnest zeal to find and follow "him of whom Moses in the law and also the prophets wrote" (1:45), they are not yet open to the glory of the Word. With the powerful image of the promise of the angels of God ascending and descending upon him that Jesus puts forth, he articulates the title that will fit his earthly mission: the Son of Man (1:51). This creates a palpable tension whereby both the disciples and the readers are ripe for revelation. With this tension in the air, Jesus and his disciples arrive in Cana. There, Jesus and his disciples attend a wedding feast where he encounters his mother and a shortage of wine (2:1–11). As a result of that initial dialogue, the mother of Jesus unconditionally accepts his covenantal challenge by extending his word to those who can put it into action using words that recall those of the Israelites at Sinai, "Whatever he might say to you, do." Through her acceptance of Jesus' challenge through words of covenant, she then becomes the model disciple in the time before Jesus' hour. For his part, Jesus begins to reveal his glory, and the symbolic backdrop of Pentecost, which is the revelation of the glory of God, reaches its climax.

As Jesus' journey through Jewish territory begins (2:12), readers hold his mother's covenant response in the background of their reading experience as the model against which all further responses to Jesus can be measured. Jesus goes up to Jerusalem for the Passover festival and, standing amid what he sees to be a hotbed of commerce in the temple, commands, "Stop making my Father's house a marketplace!" (2:16). Then, in the face of the stubbornness of "the Jews," as Jesus challenges, "Destroy this temple and in three days I will raise it up" (2:19), readers recognize their refusal to understand Jesus' symbolic challenge as a rejection of this covenantal relationship (2:13–22). The hope found in the disciples is based in the narrator's foreshadowing assertion of their remembrance and belief. When Jesus speaks to Nicodemus of the love of God for the world and the spiritual birth necessary to enter into relationship and see the kingdom of God (3:1–21), readers can appreciate Nicodemus's question, "How can this be?" (3:9) as openness to the covenant of belief in the word of Jesus and indicating that his journey is not yet complete. When John the Baptist, the witness sent from God, appears again (3:22–36), his countercultural response to the increase of Jesus' ministry based in the covenantal imagery of the love of the true God assures readers of his full faith and the fulfillment of his mission.

As Jesus leaves Jewish territory and starts back to Galilee by way of Samaria where he meets a woman at Jacob's well and engages her in dialogue (4:1–44), his covenantal dialogue with the first woman, his mother, remains the model. The current dialogue does not progress well initially, as the woman's misunderstanding of Jesus' intentions leads her to reject his offer of the living water of eternal life with a naïve response regarding her daily chore of coming to the well (4:1–15). Jesus then takes a different tactic, questioning her in terms of her husbands, which leads to dialogue about covenantal claims of ancestry, worship, and eventually her knowledge of the Messiah (4:16–25). Her claim opens the door for Jesus' own christological claim, "I am" (4:26). As Jesus' disciples arrive, she goes to share her discovery but reveals the partial nature of her faith journey by her still-questioning words, "Come and see a man who told me everything I have done! Could this one be the Messiah?" (4:29). The Samaritan villagers then provide the full response to Jesus, modeled by his mother at Cana, when the narrator remarks, "And many more believed because of his word" and they themselves claim that he is "truly the Savior of the world" (4:41–42).

When Jesus returns to Cana, his covenantal activity is brought to the foreground once again (4:45–54). When he is engaged in dialogue by a royal official who is described as a man and father with a sick boy, readers are ready for Jesus' challenge to the authenticity of his faith. The covenantal nature of the royal official's response is revealed in the similarity of this entire scene with that of the first sign at Cana, including the father's belief in the word of Jesus and obedience to his command. Like that first one, this sign is confirmed by unwitting witnesses, and belief in Jesus spreads through the covenant household of faith as the narrator confirms that this journey from Cana to Cana, inaugurated by the unconditional acceptance of the Jewish mother of Jesus to his covenantal challenge, has come full circle with this Gentile father.

The Cana to Cana narrative of John 2—4 is thus an educational journey that teaches the nature of authentic faith. As we arrive at 4:54, the ministry of Jesus has come a long way. All those whom he has encountered have been affected by his word and deed, some changed forever (John the Baptist, the Samaritan villagers), others resolutely unchanged ("the Jews"), and still others slowly making the first steps along their own journeys of faith (Nicodemus, the Samaritan woman). Jesus, too, has been affected by these encounters. His interactions with people along the way are marked by his human experience of them and with them. As his fame spreads, he is brought into contact with more and more people. Yet, in these ensuing encounters, he pushes harder for those he meets to believe in his word, despite that renown. His disciples, too, are journeying, watching, and remembering (2:11–12, 22; 3:22; 4:27–38). This is a dynamic process of ever-challenging and deepening belief in the Word, based in covenantal relationship. Readers, likewise, are making this journey along with them. The background of this journey is the language and imagery of covenant. The pattern of temporal and spatial markers across 1:19—2:12 manifests the symbolism of the Feast of Pentecost as the theological canvas of this narrative portrait.

By NT times, the revelation of the glory of God and the foundation of the covenant between God and all Israel at Sinai was linked to the Feast of Pentecost. This rich symbolic framework is the foundation upon which the encounter between Jesus and his mother at the wedding feast at Cana is built. The educational journey that follows this revelatory event is a journey of discovery and ever-deepening understanding of the covenantal process of belief in the Word that empowers all who encounter Jesus to become children of God. The fullness of this covenant will not be revealed until the very hour of the true glory of God that was introduced in the first dialogue in Cana of Galilee, Jesus' passion and crucifixion (19:16b–37; see 2:1–12). But this hour has not yet arrived. Jesus has much yet to testify and teach about himself and his relationship with the Father. His work in Jerusalem has only just begun. His ministry now turns to the rest of the major feasts of Judaism, where God's covenantal relationship with Israel is remembered and experienced as ongoing and present in its daily life (John 5—10). With the temple as his background, Jesus now places himself in dialogue with "the Jews" so that he might render those feasts christological and thereby give himself as the covenantal fulfillment of the presence of God in their midst. Readers, too, must make their way, along with Jesus and his disciples, from this initial educational journey of faith through the christological experience of the feasts of Israel.

Jesus and the Jewish Festivals (John 5—10)

In biblical literature, the feasts of Israel are presented as celebrations that recall God's saving action in the past and render that action present in the current community. In the Torah, Leviticus 23 narrates God's appointment of the feasts through Moses. The celebration of a Jewish feast is a *zikaron*, a "memorial" (Lev 23:24), of God's past active presence in the lives of his chosen people. Celebrating the liturgy of the feast manifests God's presence among the people in the current age. The celebration of the feasts of Israel was therefore also intimately connected with the experience of God's covenantal action in and with creation. The narrative imagery of covenant forms the backdrop of all that Jesus says and does in this segment of his public life.

The Gospel gives evidence, which we will discuss in more detail in the conclusion, that the Johannine Christians had been expelled from the synagogues (see 9:22; 12:42; 16:2). If so, they were not simply being excluded from these celebrations (a social experience), they may have felt that they were losing contact with the God of creation and God's saving action in history (a religious experience). As believers in the saving action of the Christ event, they were taught that covenantal relationship with God is engendered through the word of Jesus (see 2:1—4:54). But this presents another problem: What about these feasts and the experience of God's presence they facilitate? Not only does the Fourth Evangelist have to care for the community members pastorally because they are no longer in that world; he also has to show God's fidelity to them and God's continuing presence in their lives as members of the new covenantal community. This reshaping of the experience of God in the life of the community is the background for the narrator's indications of the feasts of Judaism in John 5—10 (see 5:9b; 6:4; 7:2; 10:22). Through this portion of the Book of Signs, the Evangelist therefore renders the feasts of Judaism as christological. It is Jesus the Christ who is the perfection of Jewish liturgy and theology. It is Jesus the Christ who renders God present in the ongoing lives of the community. This process began in John 2—4 in the presentation of the feast of Pentecost as the theological canvas behind the portrait of the wedding feast at Cana and the ensuing educational journey of faith from Cana to Cana. In John 5—10, the Evangelist turns to the remaining major feasts of the Jewish ritual calendar. A year's time in the narrative passes, marked temporally by the general "after these things" (5:1; 6:1; 7:1) until the culminating designation "it happened then" (10:22). Following his return to Cana (4:46–54), Jesus goes up to Jerusalem to an unnamed "feast of the Jews" (5:1) where he eventually engages in dialogue about the weekly feast of Sabbath (5:10). John 6 focuses on the spring festival of Passover (6:4). John 7 introduces an extended narrative section complete with discourse and dialogue, all set around the autumn feast of Tabernacles (7:2). The final feast that takes place in these chapters is the winter festival of Dedication (10:22). A perfection of the liturgical celebration of God's presence in the context of the fulfillment of God's plan for humankind to live in relationship as children of God through belief in the word of Jesus pervades each festival narrative and discourse. The climactic close of this segment is the revelation that God and Jesus are one (10:30).

John 5 thus begins at an unnamed feast of "the Jews" (5:1). The narrator's designation of this setting introduces themes of the next six chapters: how Jesus relates to the presence of God celebrated in the Jewish feasts and how the Johannine community is to begin to reshape its liturgical life. Readers learn that the weekly feast of Sabbath is the focus of this first narrative and discourse, as Jesus sees a man lying near the pool by the Sheep Gate in Jerusalem and heals him on the Sabbath (vv. 2–9). As part of the healing command, however, Jesus instructs the man to carry his pallet. The healed man begins with full faith in his compliant response, thereby breaking Sabbath law, becomes fragile as he shifts responsibility, then falls away as he turns to stand with "the Jews" and accepts their authority and their categories, as well as the application of both of these to his life (vv. 10–16). For his part, Jesus remains constant and in control ("My father is working still, and I work," v. 17). What Jesus claims in these verses about his relationship to God and Sabbath is essential to further understand who he is and the revelation of God that he brings. Jesus, as the Son of God the Father, transcends human bonds historically and legally (vv. 19–24). The Sabbath was established for rest because God rested, but the sun keeps rising and babies continue to be born. Therefore, God rests save for two primary functions: giving life and judging. The custom of the day associated sin with death, but Jesus shows an authority as life-giver and judge (vv. 25–30) and hints that he has been granted functions traditionally restricted to God (vv. 31–47). He transcends Sabbath law without destroying or replacing it by fulfilling the roles the Father has given him. "The Jews" reject this claim and challenge to believe him right away and begin to seek "all the more to kill him" (v. 18). The scene comes to an end with no resolution. Jesus' accusers make no verbal response to his challenge. The healed man does not seem to have understood a challenge was even at stake. The chapter thus serves to introduce this series of christological perfections of the Jewish feasts within their covenantal contexts.

The expression "after these things" (6:1) once again marks a new temporal setting that allows for a new geographical setting as well. The narrator informs us that, as the feast of Passover drew near, Jesus and his disciples, followed by a sign-seeking, large crowd, went to the other side of the Sea of Galilee (vv. 1–4). All this takes place as Jesus positions himself "on a mountain." These introductory remarks bring to mind the covenant-making event at Sinai (Exod 19—24) and lead into the miraculous feeding of five thousand people with a boy's provision of five barley loaves and two fish (vv. 5–15). The crowds clamor to make Jesus king by force, leading him to withdraw. He later comes to his disciples by night across the sea during the storm (vv. 16–21). The narrator then re-gathers the characters and details the scene once again (vv. 22–24) to prepare for the Bread of Life discourse (vv. 25–59). In these verses, Jesus establishes himself as the true bread from heaven who will give life so that those who eat of it will neither hunger nor thirst. When "the Jews" murmur about his origin and ability to speak in this way, Jesus responds with further claims of his heavenly origin by speaking of his body as the living bread, the perfection of God's wilderness gift of manna at Sinai. More questioning by "the Jews" only prompts Jesus to press further, establishing the Son of Man, sent from the Father, whose flesh and blood sustain life, as the one in whom they can abide forever.

In the extended narrative and dialogue of John 6, Jesus thus stands on a mountain in the countryside of Galilee during the time of Passover and reveals himself to be the true bread from heaven. He is the perfection of the gift of God to Israel in the Sinai wilderness that gives life to all who partake of his offer of himself (vv. 25–40). In response to the murmuring of the crowd regarding his identity, Jesus claims, "I am the bread of life" (v. 48). Using the ceremonial imagery of eating and drinking the covenant meal—and offering himself as that meal—Jesus challenges the characters in the story, both the crowds and those who claim to be his disciples, to open themselves to the ongoing revelation of God in himself and into eternal relationship with him (vv. 52–59). With these provocative words, Jesus verbally challenges the crowds further than he has thus far in his public ministry, to the very limits of their religious worldview. The enormity

44

of the progression of Jesus' public challenge in these verses is borne out by the varying responses narrated in verses 60–71. "The Jews" and many disciples are unable to go any further in their response to Jesus as the ongoing revelation of God. For in their worldview, Moses, the manna, and Torah are the end of God's gifts and they choose to remain with the former gift, rejecting the fullness of the gift of the truth. As a result, "When many of his disciples heard it, they said, 'This is a hard saying, who can listen to it?'" (v. 60). Jesus acknowledges their limits of belief, and for the first time in the narrative, many of his disciples turn back (v. 66). The crisis created by the word of Jesus begins to take its toll. Jesus turns to "the Twelve" and puts the decision to them, "Do you also wish to go away?" Simon Peter begins to take a leadership position and responds on behalf of the disciples by making a public confession of their growing belief in Jesus as well as their determination to follow him: "Lord, to whom shall we go? You have the words of eternal life. We have come to believe and to know that you are the Holy One of God" (vv. 68–69). The narrator advises, however, that the disciples are only beginning to understand the full ramifications of such belief in the origins and destiny of Jesus, as he introduces readers to Judas Iscariot, "who was going to betray him" (v. 71). These words of acceptance are thus marked with the foreboding of trial and betrayal. In the final words of this episode, Jesus reveals that intrinsic in the choice of his own is the path to the hour of his suffering and glory (v. 70). The events and dialogue of John 6 lead to a turning point in the narrative, as the audience participates, not only in the mass exodus of the crowds from uncritical following of Jesus, but also in the revelation of the beginning of the end of the Son of Man's earthly mission. Even in the midst of professions of faith, the tension of a future betrayal mounts and the shadow of a violent death begins to loom.

The narrative tempo shifts again with the marker "after these things" and the information that Jesus remained in Galilee, for "the Jews were seeking to kill him" in Judea (7:1). Further, the entirety of John 7:1—10:21 takes place in the context of the Jewish festival of Tabernacles (v. 2). This lengthy unit falls into two major sections once Jesus goes up to Jerusalem (7:2–13). In the first section, Jesus uses the backdrop of Tabernacles as the canvas for his teaching of himself as the living water and light of the world that brings about the integration and fulfillment of the Jewish scriptural history (7:14—8:59). The second section focuses on Jesus healing a man born blind. This sign provides for an extended discussion of Jesus' identity by others as well as Jesus' own self-identification as the Good Shepherd, who will lay down his life for his own (9:1—10:21).

As a literary piece, John 7—8 is one of the most difficult movements in the Gospel narratives. When the dialogue between Jesus and the Jewish leaders and the crowds in the temple during the feast of Tabernacles reaches its climax (8:31–59), it is the most passionate, even vitriolic, conflict narrated in the Gospels. Both sides of the encounter are very heated: "The Jews" accuse Jesus of having a demon (v. 48), and Jesus calls them children of the devil, the father of lies (vv. 42–47). The entire encounter forces the people (and the audience) to begin to make decisions about where they stand in the mounting christological conflict between Jesus and the Jewish authorities. The gulf separating Jesus and "the Jews" at the feast of Tabernacles is a profound *closedness*. The audience of John 7—8 has the Prologue resonating in their ears as they listen to Jesus' teaching in this most intense segment of his ministry. They have information about Jesus and the glory of God's action in and for the sake of the world through the covenantal gift of truth in Jesus. Thus, when the audience experiences Jesus verbalizing what God is doing through him in the tenor of his own voice, there is room for his word. "The Jews," who stand outside the world of the Prologue, are ultimately not *open* to hearing and seeing God the Father in the voice and person of Jesus the Son. Although many can come to a partial faith in the messianic mission of Jesus when it rings familiar to their long-standing religious system, they cannot take root and abide in his word when he reveals the full implications of the life-giving truth of his messiahship. They can neither appreciate nor participate in the openness of the very figures of their religious history to which they appeal. Thus, even as authentic progeny, they choose to remain outside the covenantal realm of the children of God, for children hear the word of their Father and do as their Father does, as manifest in the Son the Father gives to them.

For his part, Jesus stands in the temple area in the midst of the feast of Tabernacles that celebrates the experience of God's care for the children of Israel in the wilderness at Sinai and presents himself as the covenantal mediation of the experience of God's life-giving care now and forever. As the participants in the Tabernacles celebration relive their ancestors' experience of God through rituals of water and light, Jesus shows himself to be the living water and true light that reveals God to all who would open themselves to him and take root in his word, thus empowering them to become the covenantal children of God. In the dialogue of Tabernacles, Jesus reveals that all that is accomplished in that annual feast is perfected in him through the covenantal love between the true Son and the living Father, now and forever.

These extended scenes of dialogue and narrative in the context of the celebration of God's covenantal gift of Torah that escalate to violent controversy are the point in this section where "the Jews" begin to come to a decision about Jesus. The Evangelist narrates their ultimate response of rejection to his challenge of abiding in his word as they attempt to stone the Son of Man for blasphemy (8:59). The controversy continues as Jesus heals a man born blind, and the Evangelist gives a glimpse into the conflict of his own time as the threat of expulsion from the synagogue to those who follow Jesus is articulated (9:1–41). Jesus affirms that acceptance and belief have their own rewards, for he is the Good Shepherd who lays down his life for his sheep (10:1–18). Jesus' extended use of shepherd imagery to describe himself resonates with God's self-characterization in the words of the prophet Ezekiel. Israel's failure to "know" God resulted in it being convicted of breach of covenant, the result for which was exile (for example, Ezek 12:15–16). Once God speaks of establishing a covenant with Israel anew, he calls himself the "shepherd" who will seek out and care for his sheep (Ezek 34:15–16) and "make with them a covenant of peace" so that "they will know that I am God" (Ezek 34:25–31). By employing the shepherd imagery at the conclusion of the events at the feast of Tabernacles, Jesus echoes the covenantal declarations of God in Ezekiel. He identifies himself first as the gate (v. 9) through which anyone can enter the fold of the sheep of God, then as the Good Shepherd (vv. 11, 14), who is known by his own and God the Father (vv. 14b–15a).

The final temporal and festival marker of this section is found at John 10:22, when the narrator indicates that "at that time the festival of Dedication occurred in Jerusalem." This relatively brief scene (twenty-one verses) closes the feasts section by focusing on Jesus' teaching. These few verses, however, are important for understanding the conclusion to this larger section that moves through the annual feasts of Judaism. The narrator designates that it is now winter and Jesus is walking in the portico of Solomon during the festival of Dedication (the month of Kislev: November–December). This celebration relives the experience of the Jewish people rededicating the temple after the desecration—the erection and forced worship of a statue of Zeus by the Greek King Antiochus IV Epiphanes—was demolished and the altar was cleansed following the successful Maccabean revolt of 167–164 BC (1 Macc 1—4). Solomon's portico, the oldest colonnade on the eastern face of the temple, is a fitting backdrop for this final confrontation, since it occurs during the festival commemorating Jewish resistance to blasphemy, idolatry, and apostasy. Speculation about the messiahship of Jesus has been in the air for some time and "the Jews" seek to put an end to it: "If you are the Messiah, tell us plainly" (v. 24).

Jesus takes up the shepherding imagery of his previous discourse to identify himself once again as the Shepherd (vv. 25–30). He presses far beyond his interrogators' messianic imagery by presenting his oneness with God: "I and the Father are one" (v. 30). Even as "the Jews" take up stones against him for his perceived blasphemy (v. 31), Jesus responds to their unspoken accusation by appealing to Torah specifically, Scripture generally, and his own divine works (vv. 32–38). But his final covenantal assertion, "that you may know and understand that the Father is in me and I am in the Father," falls on uncomprehending ears as "the Jews" attempt to arrest him. However, his hour, now closer, has not yet come and Jesus once again escapes their hands (v. 39). This segment comes to a close with Jesus returning across the Jordan where "many began to believe in him" (vv. 41–42).

The symbolic rhetoric of Jesus' dialogues throughout these chapters flows from the well of the OT covenant metaphor as over and again Jesus issues the challenge to embark upon a journey of faith that will bring everyone he encounters into covenant relationship with him. The action his speech evokes in his dialogue partners is a movement toward him or a turning away from him in acceptance or rejection of his challenge of covenant relationship in the family of God. Throughout, he verbally points to himself as the revelation of the Word of God who gives this gift of truth to those who would become children of God. The narrative imagery of the feasts of Israel, all of which are intimately connected to the experience of God's covenantal action in and with creation, forms the backdrop of all that Jesus says and does in this major segment of his public life. The identity of Jesus is revealed in his relationship to God who is celebrated through these festivals. He reveals a unique Father–Son relationship, a relationship of family, that itself emanates the imagery of covenant. Further, the Father has sent the Son for the purpose of summoning all the children of God to himself. These children know the voice of the Son and respond as sheep to a shepherd, gathering and abiding in the light of life that he gives. As Jesus moves through the feasts of Israel, he voices a continual clarion call of this invitational challenge to covenant, heard by the disciples, the crowds, "the Jews," and the reader. The ever-increasing intensity of both his covenantal rhetoric and the potential consequences imposed by those who reject his self-revelatory challenge marks the progress of the Gospel story. Nonetheless, this lengthy portion of Jesus' public ministry draws to a close in belief rather than condemnation. A final reference to the truthful witness of John allows the Evangelist to provide a moment of reflection for the audience. The words of the Prologue resonate as the testimony of Jesus reconstitutes "his own" not restricted to ethnic Judaism but as all those who receive and believe in him (10:42; see 1:11–12). With these suggestions, readers move with Jesus to glory.

Transitions of Faith: The Arrival of the Hour of Jesus (John 11—12)

Chapters 11—12 of the Fourth Gospel are crucial to the theological flow of this good news, because they move the narrative out of the ministry and into the cross. In the words and actions of Jesus, the Evangelist culminates the themes of life and light that have permeated his Gospel from their introduction in the Prologue (1:3–5). The entrance into a new segment in the story is indicated by the introduction of a new setting (Bethany, 11:1), and new characters (the siblings Mary, Martha, and Lazarus, whom Jesus loves, 11:5). These first verses also reveal that Jesus' role as the life-giver who sheds light on those who walk with him will be perfected (11:7–15). At the same time, the narrator's foreshadowing aside that Mary is the one who anointed Jesus raises a note of tension about the events to come and the death that is impending (11:2; see 12:1–8). Although it is Lazarus whose physical life is at stake, the intricately constructed narrative that unfolds emphasizes the faith journeys of Jesus' friends, Mary and Martha, as he challenges them to see in him not the culmination of a historical religious system but the perfection of life in the spirit through the covenantal relationship of believing in God. Although Jesus does give life to Lazarus, and many of "the Jews began to believe in him" (v. 45), his gift of life serves to render his own death all the more imminent. At the pinnacle of irony, the high priest, Caiaphas, prophesies that this "one man" would "die instead of the people" (v. 50). The narrator steps in to clarify the prophetic word so that the audience can grasp that Jesus was about to die, "to gather into one the dispersed children of God" (v. 52), such that, even in the face of death, Jesus gives the gift of life in covenantal relationship as a child of God to all who call on his name (vv. 53–54; see 1:12). Indeed, Jesus' death will bring about the restoration and union of the covenant people, a reconstituted Israel, as the true children of God.

The arrival of the final festival of the Jews of this story is announced at 11:55. The Passover is at hand and the many who have arrived in Jerusalem are abuzz with what might occur. The tension is high and the crisis is at hand (11:56–57). This is confirmed as John 12 begins and Mary's foretold anointing of Jesus with perfumed oil comes to pass. It is this intimate scene of burial preparation that lies behind Jesus' heralded entry into Jerusalem (vv. 12–15). This event confounds Jesus' disciples, but remains with them and in their memory when Jesus is glorified

(v. 16). The narrator steps in again, however, to warn the reader of the superficial sign-oriented nature of the faith of the people that may not abide (vv. 17–18). The triumph of Jesus' entry into Jerusalem for the Passover may also prove fleeting. The hour that will bring about the crisis of these faith journeys in the glorification of Jesus is foreshadowed with the exclamation of the Pharisees that "the world has gone after him" (v. 19), and precipitated by the arrival of the Greeks who seek to see Jesus (vv. 20–22). As he announces the arrival of his hour, Jesus speaks of love, service, and honor, in relationship with the Father, but his soul is troubled (vv. 24–27). The hour of his glorification is also an hour of distress for Jesus who, despite his foreknowledge, is no less affected by his mission as the Son of Man in the world. He confirms his mission through a prayer of determination and is acknowledged and affirmed by the voice from heaven (v. 28). The discussion among the people that results from this voice leads Jesus to affirm his desire to "draw all people" to himself. In the covenantal language of the family of God, he urges, "While you have the light, believe in the light, so that you may become children of the light" (vv. 35–36a). However, in fulfillment of the word of Isaiah who saw his glory, Jesus departs from the people, who are then left to their own crises: the glory of God or the fear of being put out of the synagogue and the world they know (vv. 36b–43). Those who choose the former accept Jesus' covenantal challenge and are empowered to become children of God. Those who choose the latter reject Jesus' challenge and remain the progeny of the world.

Jesus then cries out his final words in the public sphere, giving a climactic voice to the themes of mission and light first introduced in the Prologue (vv. 44–50). These verses resonate with the covenantal themes of Deuteronomy. The words of God are now uttered by the prophet like Moses incarnate in Jesus the Son of God (v. 49; Deut 18:15, 18–19), and these directives set the pattern of daily life for the people (vv. 47–48; Deut 8:3), and give life to Israel (v. 50; Deut 32:45–47). The word of God, spoken through Jesus, sums up the covenant obligations of the believer. With the intimacy of the relationship between God the Father and Jesus the Son, as well as their shared desire to extend this covenantal relationship of family to all who would become children of God, we move to the glory of the hour of Jesus.

Teaching People to Believe

The narratives and dialogues that close Jesus' public ministry bring the themes of life and light to their peaks, as Jesus places himself in the midst of the Jewish people and reveals himself to be the resurrection and the life on the eve of the hour of his glorification. In the aftermath of the sign that Jesus performs in the raising of Lazarus, the Jewish authorities are prompted to make the final decision that Jesus must die (11:45–57). The Evangelist continues to distinguish between superficial belief and abiding in the word of Jesus that reflects the authentic faith of true children of God. Many would-be disciples continue on their journeys of faith, while the persistent unbelief of the crowds is finally confirmed (12:37). The fear of others to confess Jesus as the Messiah lest they be expelled from the synagogue is condemned by the narrator as the failing of human will (12:42–43). The audience of the Gospel finds itself in the midst of these journeys of faith. They, too, are being brought to a crisis and must determine with whom to identify as they decide the direction their own journey will take.

Jesus himself sums up his revelatory discourse in terms of the covenant obligations of the believer (12:44–50). In stark contrast to those who love human praise more than the praise of God, Jesus and those who accept him—those whom he has empowered to become the true children of God—speak out the words the Father has commanded, regardless of the earthly consequences. Jesus has been sent to save the world and those who receive him receive the gift of God, which is eternal life. As Jesus' public ministry comes to an end, he turns toward his own and the hour of his glorification, when the mission of his covenantal gift to the world will be fulfilled.

Questions for Review

1. Why is John 1:19—12:50 often called the Book of Signs? What is a sign and what does it have to do with believing in the good news of Jesus as the Messiah?

2. In John 1:19–51, the Evangelist describes the first days of Jesus. Why might he not narrate the baptism of Jesus by John? What is the role of John the Baptist in this Gospel?

3. In what ways does John 2—4 form the primary catechetical, or "instructional," section of the Gospel of John? What is the Evangelist trying to teach his audience?

4. How are belief, sin, and authentic faith characterized in this journey of encounters? In other words, how does belief in the "Word" of the Prologue play out in John 2—4 in terms of covenant?

5. Why is Jesus' traveling into Samaria something he "had" to do as part of his mission? With this in mind, identify and describe three ways the Samaritan woman at the well is symbolic of the character of the new covenant people Jesus is gathering; then conclude how Jesus can be proclaimed the "savior of the world" by the Samaritan villagers.

6. John 5—10 presents Jesus as fulfilling the purpose of the Jewish festivals. Why might this be important for the Evangelist's early Christian community?

7. In the Bread of Life discourse of John 6, Jesus uses the imagery of Moses and the Sinai covenant to teach of himself in a way that is also symbolic of the eucharistic meal. What is the covenantal connection between these images?

8. John 11—12 transitions the Gospel from the Book of Signs to the Book of Glory with the climactic sign of the raising of Lazarus and the arrival of the hour of Jesus' glorification. How is this also representative of God's new covenantal activity?

4

JESUS AND HIS OWN

Covenant in the Book of Glory

The Book of Signs has come to a close. The signs of this first half of the body of the Gospel anticipate the glory of the second half (John 13—20). Jesus' signs have drawn people in and he has taught of himself and God's promises through him, generating a crisis of faith that has pushed people to come to a decision about him. His hour has now arrived and he prepares for the glorification God will give. In turn, the action of the second half, the Book of Glory, accomplishes in reality what was anticipated in the first half. We now focus on Jesus' last discourse with and preparation of his disciples for life and leadership in the new covenant relationship (John 13—17) as well as the passion narrative as the culmination of the glorification of the Father's only Son (John 18—19). We will conclude with a look at the resurrection of the Word (John 20) and the dialogue of covenant across this portion of the story.

Introduction to the Book of Glory

The Book of Signs (John 1:19—12:50) depicts the public ministry of Jesus. His words and deeds address a wide audience and provoke a crisis of faith wherein some believe and some refuse to believe. The Book of Glory (John 13:1—20:31) can be characterized as the result of that crisis. It is addressed to the restricted audience of those who believe. This, finally, is "the hour" of his passion, crucifixion, and resurrection. These distinctions are made apparent in the first verse of this portion of the narrative (13:1). Furthermore, the Book of Glory reverses the narrative action of the Book of Signs. In that first part of the body of the Gospel, Jesus' dialogues and discourses followed and served to interpret the signs. In this second part, the Last Supper and discourse (13:1—17:26) precede the passionate action of glorification (18:1—19:42) and serve to foretell and interpret that action for the ongoing community of believers, however initially struggling and skeptical (20:1-31).

Jesus and the Last Discourse with the Disciples (John 13—17)

The form and content of the last discourse has lent itself to considerable scholarly discussion regarding its structure. Repetitions and discrepancies in sequence and content in these chapters have resulted in various approaches to interpreting the scenes narrated within them. Despite these difficulties, there is an increasing consensus that John 13—17 presents a coherent narrative unit. The structure and content of this episode begins with Jesus making God known through washing the feet of his disciples and sharing a final meal with them (13:1-38). The focus then turns to departure as Jesus promises God's abiding presence and guidance to the disciples (14:1-31). The heart of the discourse centers on a new covenant call for the disciples to abide, to love, and to be hated by the world (15:1—16:3). The remainder of the encounter revisits the earlier theme of departure, now in terms of the consequences of discipleship (16:4-33) before returning to Jesus' final prayer in which he once again makes God known by consecrating the new community (17:1-26). The overview of John 13—17 that follows highlights the covenant motif manifested in the Fourth Evangelist's story of Jesus' last meal and discourse with his disciples.

Jesus began to gather disciples in the first days of his public ministry (1:35-51). Covenant themes of chosenness, knowledge of God, and abiding relationship with God suggest that these early scenes represent the initiation of these disciples into a covenant relationship with God through Jesus. Throughout the narrative of Jesus' public ministry in John 2—12, the disciples witness and participate in the signs and mission of Jesus that call them to a decision about Jesus and about their role in his ministry. By 6:67–71, Jesus has singled out the Twelve for special status as "his own" inner circle. When he puts the question to them of whether they too will go away like so many others or remain with him, Peter answers on behalf of the disciples that they have come to "know" and to "believe" that Jesus, the Holy One of God, has the words of eternal life (vv. 68–69). From this point forward, Jesus' challenges to relationship with him become all the more potent and provocative. By the end of his public ministry, the disciples consciously choose to accompany Jesus to Judea and eventually to Jerusalem, even under the threat of death (11:16). With regard to the disciples, the narrative thus far has functioned as preparation for the final challenge that abiding relationship with Jesus brings. Once the disciples, however rough their understanding of the full ramifications of their new leadership role, confirm their resolve, the encounter culminates in the prayer that seals their covenantal relationship with Jesus and perfects their place in the new covenant tradition. This process begins with a gathering of Jesus and "his own" for a farewell meal.

MAKING GOD KNOWN: THE FOOT WASHING AND THE MORSEL (13:1–38)

John 13 introduces the themes of the last discourse and serves as a foundational element of the covenant metaphor that unfolds across these chapters. The first verses provide a solemn introduction that transitions the audience into not only the foot-washing scene but the entire second half of the Gospel. Beginning with the characterization of the disciples as Jesus' own, verses 1–3 set the scene of a covenant meal in which Jesus participates with "his own" whom he loves "to the end." Just as the OT covenant meals signify both God's choice of covenant partners and the acceptance of the covenant by those partners (Gen 26:26–30; 31:43–54; Exod 24:5–11; Deut 27:6–7), Jesus' final meal with his disciples signifies the covenantal nature of their relationship: an intimate bond of friendship, shared knowledge, and acceptance that binds them as the new family of God. The action of the foot washing symbolizes Jesus' self-sacrificing, perfecting love in relationship with the disciples (vv. 4–20). The OT narrates foot washing as a gesture of hospitality (Gen 18:4; 19:2; 24:32; 43:32; Judg 19:21; 1 Sam 25:41) and as preparation for meeting God (Exod 30:17–21). Washing in general is associated with ushering in the promise of the new covenant (Ezek 36:25–28). By washing the feet of his disciples, Jesus thus allows them to have a share in his mission and destiny in relationship with God.

The narrative that ensues from this communal meal and symbolic action provides the impetus for a new covenant commandment based on mutual love as modeled by Jesus' own humble self-sacrificing mission that will ultimately lead to glorification (vv. 21–35). The remainder of the chapter narrates three possible responses to this covenantal challenge represented in the figures and actions of Judas (vv. 2, 11, 18–20, 26–31), Peter (vv. 6–9, 36–38), and the Beloved Disciple (vv. 21–26). These responses correlate with the reactions to Jesus and his word by those he encountered throughout his public ministry. The character and action of Judas present a model of complete rejection of Jesus and the relationship he offers (see v. 30). The character, words, and actions of Peter represent a partial acceptance of Jesus. The character, words, and action of the Beloved Disciple represent total faithfulness or complete acceptance of Jesus' call to covenantal relationship (see v. 23). The Beloved Disciple comes forward in the narrative as the one who shares an intimate relationship with Jesus and the only disciple who seems to travel in lockstep with Jesus on his journey through the hour of his glorification. He begins to emerge as the disciple who is the model witness to Jesus' true destiny and meaning for the world. As the final meal between Jesus and his own comes to a close and night falls, Jesus begins to speak in earnest of the promises this covenantal relationship offers.

DEPARTURE: THE PROMISE OF GOD'S ABIDING PRESENCE AND GUIDANCE (14:1–31)

The movement of the last discourse shifts at 14:1 as the scene moves from the dialogue between Jesus and Peter (13:36–38) to a dialogue between Jesus and the disciples as a group, marked by his double use of the command to "believe" (v. 1). Alongside this belief, Jesus encourages the disciples through his urging, "Let not your hearts be troubled" (vv. 1, 27). The primary focus of this section of Jesus' discourse is the content of the promises he offers to his disciples who have entered into relationship with him. These promises correlate thematically with the covenantal promises of a renewal ceremony, including the indwelling presence of the Divine (vv. 3, 12–21, 23, 28; see Exod 25:8), the knowledge of the Divine (vv. 7, 17, 20–21, 26; see Exod 29:45–46; Lev 26:11–12), and the gift of peace (v. 27; see Isa 9:6–7; 52:7; 57:19; Ezek 34:25; 37:26; Hag 2:9). Interspersed throughout these promises Jesus offers to his disciples who are in covenant relationship with him, is a call to believe and keep the commandments of his word. All Jesus' words are encapsulated in two commandments: to believe in him (vv. 1, 10–12) and to love God (vv. 15, 21, 23–24). The entire covenantal obligation for disciples in this relationship that invokes Jesus' promises comes down to keeping these commandments. In John 15, Jesus turns to a more detailed exposition of this call.

THE NEW COVENANT CALL TO ABIDE, TO LOVE, AND TO BE HATED (15:1—16:3)

The central section of Jesus' last discourse with his disciples is united by the overarching theme of the obligations of discipleship in this covenant relationship. John 15:1–17 provides a metaphor of vine and branches that symbolically describes the covenant relationship between God and Jesus and his disciples, as well as the command to abide in Jesus and to love one another. After his initial call for departure in 14:31, Jesus uses the metaphor of the vine to describe himself, with God the Father as the vine grower. The journey of the disciples with Jesus thus far has been one of pruning and cleansing as the branches of the vine. The challenge for the disciples from this point is one of abiding in that integral relationship of the vine and vine grower. As he continues, Jesus identifies himself and his actions with the love of the Father, and therefore expands his call for the disciples to abide in his love. His explicit covenant command follows as he exhorts the disciples whom he has chosen to love one another as he has loved them. Both the description of the covenant partners as specifically "chosen" and the exhortation to keep God's commandments are integral parts of speeches that precede OT covenant-making and renewing processes (see Deut 30:16; Exod 34:11; Josh 24:14–15).

As Jesus is imparting the command to love to his chosen disciples, he also begins to speak in terms of friendship and integrates friendship with the love to which he is calling them. The OT narratives of friendship may underlie the perspective of these verses where "friendship" does not depend on the traditional or legal bonds of kinship, but rather manifests the same covenant faithfulness and steadfast love that defines God's relationship to Israel. The love and fidelity the friends show to one another mirror God's own covenant faithfulness and, as part of the scriptural heritage of the Johannine community, inform the language of abiding friendship and commandment to love in John 15. Jesus then turns to the ramifications of the abiding relationship of love and friendship to which he calls his disciples (16:1–4).

DEPARTURE: THE CONSEQUENCES OF DISCIPLESHIP (16:4–33)

Jesus shifts the focus of his discourse from the covenantal community of disciples itself to the consequences this relationship will bring as the disciples face the larger world. He first warns the disciples of the suffering and persecution they will encounter but follows his warnings with both the reasons behind the tribulation and the rewards for their perseverance. Despite the hatred and alienation the members of the community of disciples may experience, they must not falter. Although the community will be accused of apostasy, it is the opponents of Jesus and his community who have not remained faithful to the covenant relationship with God for they do not know the Father (see Exod 29:45–46; Jer 9:24; Isa 1:2). The reward and consolation that Jesus gives to his community for standing fast in the midst of this tribulation is the gift of the Advocate, the Evangelist's particular title for the Holy Spirit (15:26–27; 16:4–24).

Jesus reveals the purpose of these consequences to abiding in relationship with him to be strengthening so that they might be prevented from falling away on their journey. The ultimate reward for their perseverance is the gift of the Advocate, who is judge of the world, and who will guide the disciples into the truth the covenant relationship manifests (see Pss 25:5, 9; 143:10). In the end, their hearts will rejoice and their joy will be complete. With these words of challenge and consolation, Jesus now turns to his disciples for their response. The disciples then articulate their acceptance of the relationship including all its promises, obligations, and consequences through their profession of belief in Jesus and his word (vv. 29–30). Despite its brevity, this section is a climactic moment in Jesus' ongoing relationship with his disciples. Both the disciples in the story and the subsequent audience of the story are challenged by Jesus to decide definitively either for or against him in terms of the belief and love that have been the primary concerns of his discourse thus far. The first part of this section narrates the ultimate self-revelation of Jesus to his disciples, while the second part provides the disciples' response to him: their profession of faith as a group.

Jesus frames this teaching with reference to his hour (vv. 25–26a, 32–33) in which the disciples will face the consequences of their relationship with Jesus and yet also come into their own as children of God. In its core, Jesus reaffirms his origins and destiny with the Father, an intimacy that will also be shared with the disciples who love and believe in Jesus (vv. 26b–28). For their part, the disciples respond as a group to Jesus' challenge of relationship. Their emphasis on "now," what they "know," and what they "believe" about Jesus and his origins affirms in covenantal overtones that they are responding to the commandments with which Jesus has challenged them (vv. 29–30). Although they may not yet fully understand the mission of Jesus and his pending return to the Father, this acknowledgment of a commitment to God is integral to the covenant ceremonies of the OT (see Exod 24:3, 7; Josh 24:21–24), and is followed by a covenant-making ritual. Jesus' concluding words emphasize his power over the world and his ability to grant peace in the face of persecution.

MAKING GOD KNOWN: JESUS' FINAL PRAYER (17:1–26)

Jesus' last discourse concludes with a prayer through which Jesus consecrates the disciples as the firstfruits of his covenantal community. This theological climax seals the initiation process for the disciples into the light of new life. Jesus begins by entreating the Father to bring about the glorification of the Son (vv. 1–5). He then affirms that the disciples have believed in God's self-revelation in Jesus the Son (vv. 6–8). From this point, Jesus prays to the Father on behalf of these and all future disciples (v. 9). His entreaties include the keeping of the disciples in the name of the Father (vv. 10–16), and the consecration of them in the truth (vv. 17–19). The covenant theology of the OT associates knowing God's name with the realization of God's covenant relationship with Israel in the age to come (Isa 52:6). The Prologue of the Gospel of John associated the "children of God" with those who receive Jesus, who is full of the gift of truth, and believe in his name (1:12). Here in this final prayer on behalf of his disciples, Jesus acknowledges that they have received his gift of truth and consecrates them in the name of the Father. They are the firstfruits of the community of the children of God. In verse 20, Jesus moves beyond the disciples at the table with him to all who do or will believe through their word. He therefore closes the prayer with his vision for the new covenant community based in unity through the supplication that all the disciples may be one (vv. 21–26). This oneness is based on mutual abiding in the covenant relationship of God's love, which empowers them to take on the leadership role in the new community Jesus has prepared for them.

Jesus' prayer concludes the lengthy section of Jesus' last meal and discourse with his disciples. His time for teaching and building a covenant relationship with his own in this world must end so that the fullness of his hour of glorification may arrive. Through the entirety of John 13—17, the Evangelist reinterprets the covenant motif springing from different OT traditions in order to redefine and establish the identity of his community as the children of God. Only now can Jesus turn toward the hour of his passion and his glorification.

The Passion Narrative: The Covenantal Dialogue of the Cross (John 18—19)

The preservation and telling of the passion story must have had its beginnings in the earliest development of the church. In the Jewish tradition from which the Gospel arose, messiahs do not get crucified. Thus, the earliest church had to handle this historical fact both for its own identity and for its missionary purposes. Each evangelist gives his own perspective to illustrate his particular theology, but they all tell the same story with the same plotlines: the arrest, a Jewish trial process, a Roman trial process, the crucifixion, burial, and an empty tomb (see Matt 26—27, Mark 14—15, Luke 22—23). Distinctive in the passion narrative of the Gospel according to John (18—19), however, is that Jesus is always in control of his destiny. In addition, a strong focus on the disciples continues from the last discourse (13—17).

The cross is presented in John as the highest human experience (contrary to typical understanding). God exalts Jesus (3:14, 8:28, 14:32) in this "lifting up" on the cross. This same phenomenon of circumventing human understanding and expectation has appeared in the Evangelist's use of the term *glory* (1:14; 2:11; 5:41, 44; 7:18; 8:50, 54; 9:24; 11:4, 40; 12:41, 43; 17:5, 22, 24). The glory of God and the means by which Jesus is glorified (through his crucifixion) flows from the Evangelist's understanding of revelation. For the Fourth Evangelist, God so loved the world that he handed over his only Son (3:16). This handing over is an incredible act of love. Further articulation of this self-gift in love was presented in the last discourse as the revelation of God that Jesus brings and the power to become children of God that he offers (13—17)—for Jesus is the Son given to the world and who loved his own to the end (13:1). The glory of God and God's glorification of Jesus lies in this gift of the Son that begins with the incarnation (1:1–18) but is not complete until he is lifted up on the cross (see Jesus' final words on the cross, "It is finished"; 19:30).

Across John 18—19 the narrative of the passion of Jesus moves through five distinct geographical locations: the garden across the Kidron valley (18:1–11); the house of Annas, the father-

62

in-law of the high priest (18:12–27); the Roman praetorium (18:28—19:16a); Golgotha, the Place of the Skull (19:16b–37); and the new garden of Jesus' burial (19:38–42). As Jesus moves to each new location, the narrator describes the place as well as the characters and activity that are involved. Therefore, the drama of the Johannine passion narrative can be divided into five acts through these changes in location. In addition, the narrative acts begin and end in a garden, first as Jesus is confronted by his enemies and finally as he is buried by his friends. Similarly, the interrogation process of Jesus before his enemies in the second act is countered by the further formation of his own community in the fourth act. All of this action turns on the central encounter at the Roman praetorium between Jesus and Pilate, which concludes with Pilate handing Jesus over to be crucified. The flow of the passion narrative thus focuses on the nature of kingship and of God's covenantal gift of truth through Jesus at its crux.

JESUS IS ARRESTED BY HIS ENEMIES IN A GARDEN (18:1–11)

Act 1 begins with Jesus in a garden (18:1) surrounded quickly by enemies who appear by dark (vv. 2–3), an odd collusion between Rome and "the Jews" that continues through this process. Judas, the betrayer, leads the arresting party that is equipped with lanterns, torches, and weapons. The irony is that when Judas left Jesus, it became truly night for him (13:30), and now he must carry artificial light. Jesus, "knowing everything," assumes the lead in the interrogation (v. 4). In terms that resonate with his first words to his disciples, Jesus asks the arresting party, "Who are you seeking?" (vv. 4, 7). Here Jesus' question is explicitly self-referencing. The question of his identity has been asked and answered repeatedly over the course of his public ministry. His disciples indicate that they are satisfied with his response at the end of his last discourse (16:29–30). "The Jews," by contrast, have either misunderstood or explicitly rejected his responses. "Knowing all," it is with a certain irony that Jesus asks his arresting party this question now. Their response of "Jesus the Nazorean" (vv. 5, 7) results in the "I am"—the self-revelation of Jesus in the face of the collusion of his enemies in the world (vv.

6, 8). The word of Jesus thus begins to come to completion even in this first act. For his part, Peter just begins his journey through the passion as he tries to fulfill his own promise to Jesus (v. 10; see 13:36–38) but is thwarted as Jesus speaks to him in terms of his destiny: "Shall I not drink the cup which the Father has given me?" (v. 11). Although Peter's response is not recorded, his behavior in the succeeding acts shows that his self-understanding has been thrown such that he must commence his own journey of faith through Jesus' passion and resurrection before he can regain his sense of mission in the community of disciples.

Jesus Is Interrogated by "the Jews"—Condemnation (18:12–27)

Following introductory verses that describe the change of place and introduce new characters, the narrative of the Jewish hearing process is framed by the continuation of the journey of Peter, who models the struggle of the early Christians in proclaiming identity in Jesus (vv. 15–18, vv. 25–27). Within the frame of Peter's denials, Jesus claims that he has spoken openly (vv. 19–24). These scenes exemplify the frailty of the new covenant community and its propensity to falter even as it struggles to find its way and identity in a hostile world. The collusion of Jesus' enemies that bands together and arrests him now binds and leads him to Annas, the father-in-law of the high priest, Caiaphas, for interrogation. This process, the narrator implicitly reminds the audience, is bringing to fulfillment the prophecy of Caiaphas that "one man should die for the people" (v. 14; see 11:49–51). As Peter utters his third denial of Jesus, the act closes with the cockcrow. The word of Jesus continues to be fulfilled as the narrative of his passion hurtles toward its inevitable climax (v. 27; see 13:38).

Jesus Stands before Pilate—The Challenge of Truth (18:28—19:16a)

Jesus' time with Caiaphas is not narrated and the next act begins with Jesus led from the house of Caiaphas to the praetorium to stand trial before Pilate (18:28). The act of Jesus' Roman

trial unfolds in seven scenes (18:29—19:15) as Pilate moves outside and inside the praetorium to speak with "the Jews" who
refuse to come inside for fear of defilement and to speak with
Jesus who has been handed over to him for crimes against the
state. The surreal scenes of the Roman governor flitting back and
forth between the accusers and the accused, seemingly trying to
assuage both parties, emulates physically Pilate's own wavering
mental ambivalence on the charge of "the Jews" and the challenge
of the person of Jesus who stands before him discussing kingship
and truth. The truth of Jesus as King is diminished neither by
Pilate's questioning and scourging nor by "the Jews'" manipula-
tive accusing and mocking. Indeed, only in the Johannine narrative does Jesus go to the cross dressed as a king. The narrative of
Jesus' passion turns on Pilate's inexorable decision: "Then he
handed him over to them to be crucified" (19:16a). This act is
thus the core of the passion narrative by way of a distinctive dialogue between Jesus, Pilate, and "the Jews" that focuses on kingship and truth. As Pilate investigates the crime set before him and
wavers between the accusers and accused, he is stopped momen-
tarily by his own question on the nature of truth.

We will briefly explore this dialogue and its effect on the
underlying covenantal metaphor of the Gospel. Of these seven
core scenes and their narrative frame, only one scene, 19:1–3,
contains no verb of motion and no dialogue. In this scene inside
the praetorium, Jesus is crowned, dressed as a king, and ironically
proclaimed: "Hail, the King of the Jews" (v. 3). This narration and
ironic proclamation of the kingship of Jesus becomes the scene
around which the entire Roman trial narrative turns. The truth of
the kingship of Jesus and how this affects and is affected by Pilate,
"the Jews," and Jesus' own life and mission are all at stake in this
narrative. The dramatic techniques of the Fourth Evangelist thus
reach their peak in the Johannine account of the Roman trial. The
effect of the refusal of "the Jews" to enter the praetorium at the
onset of the trial is to send Pilate shuttling back and forth
between Jesus and his accusers, acting on two stages as it were, a
front stage and a rear stage. This staging enhances the drama of
the narrative and ensures that "the Jews" do not hear Jesus' revelatory dialogues with Pilate. At the same time, it portrays the

human predicament in which many of the Gospel's readers might find themselves, where they must choose between Jesus and the world. The two stages also ensure that Pilate is the only figure who appears in every scene. Nonetheless, Jesus himself, and the nature of his kingship, continue to occupy center stage. Jesus knows all and even controls the dialogue of the trial. Indeed, Pilate and his ability to recognize the truth is what seems to be on trial. This is the covenantal aspect of the unfolding drama of the passion narrative in the Fourth Gospel. Jesus, the bearer of the gift of truth that fulfills the gift of the Law (1:14, 17), in the hour of his glorification places himself before Pilate to bear witness one last time to the truth (18:37). Pilate's response determines where he stands in the new covenant community. In this vein, renowned biblical scholar Raymond Brown notes that the "real question is not what will happen to Jesus who controls his own destiny, but whether Pilate will betray himself by bowing to the outcry of the very people he is supposed to govern (19:12). The price he exacts from them by way of an insincere allegiance to Caesar (19:15) is a face-saving device for a man who knows the truth about Jesus but failed to bear witness to it (18:36–37)."[1]

Across this act, Jesus and his kingship stand at center stage. In addition, Jesus' kingship expresses God's kingship, and thus the rejection of Jesus by "the Jews" is equivalent to rejection of God. Furthermore, the mission of Jesus which manifests his kingship consists in bearing witness to the truth and is inaugurated through his sacrificial death. Biblical scholar Wayne Meeks notes that just as the Good Shepherd is the one who "lays down his life for the sheep," so the "exaltation" of the king consists in his being "lifted up" on the cross.[2] Jesus' various roles and functions across the Gospel thus begin to coalesce in this Roman trial. The Son of Man whose kingship consists of giving and bearing witness to the truth takes his stand on behalf of "his own" by issuing his final challenge before the powers of the world (18:37; see 1:14–16). Pilate, the representative of the state and all worldly power dis-

---

1. Raymond E. Brown, "The Passion according to John: Chapters 18 and 19." *Worship* 49 (1975): 130.

2. Wayne A. Meeks, *The Prophet-King: Moses Traditions and the Johannine Christology*, NovTSup 14 (Leiden: Brill, 1967), 80–81.

misses his challenge and final offer of truth (18:38) and ultimately forsakes this truth for political security (19:12–16a). But this too, is part of the mission of the Son of Man in order that he be "lifted up" (18:32; see 12:32) and by dying, "gather into one the scattered children of God" (11:52; see 1:12; 19:11).

"The Jews" and their representatives also have a major role in the process of the Roman trial. Throughout the Gospel, "the Jews" have been the Evangelist's representative characters for "the world" and its rejection of God's revelation in Jesus. By this point in the Gospel, "the Jews" have already proved themselves closed to the revelation of God in Jesus and have soundly rejected any covenantal challenge and offer of the gift of truth that the person and mission of Jesus brings. Their startling proclamation, "We have no king but Caesar!" (19:15), that brings the trial to its bitter end (19:16a) and is also uttered just as the observance of Passover begins (19:14), is not just a rejection of Jesus but a renunciation of the fundamental profession of Israel to have no king but God. Their failure, according to the Evangelist, is both a religious one and a political one as they reject Jesus (18:30–32; 19:6–7, 14–15) and choose to have Barabbas, the insurgent, released (18:39–40). Their journey of rejection of the gift of truth that has spanned the Gospel is completed here before the Roman state. At the very hour the Passover lambs are being led to the slaughter, Jesus Christ, the Lamb of God, is handed over for crucifixion.

The final character in the Roman trial narrative to be discussed is the only new character to the Fourth Gospel: Pontius Pilate, the Roman governor. Because he is a character just introduced to this narrative and his authority renders his action decisive for the remainder of the story, it behooves readers to pay particular attention to him. Pilate's interaction with "the Jews" outside the praetorium is openly hostile and the two parties stand in clear opposition. However, his interaction with Jesus inside the praetorium is more complex. On the practical level, readers might understand these dialogues between Jesus and Pilate as a model for the Johannine community's dealings with Roman officials. On the covenantal level, Pilate's dialogues with Jesus do affect Jesus and where he stands in the narrative, but they also affect Pilate and where he stands in relation to the gift of truth that forms the basis for the entire Gospel story.

In their first dialogue inside the praetorium (18:33–38a), Jesus reveals himself as a king whose kingdom is not of the world, but is nonetheless in the world (v. 36). Jesus' role in establishing this kingdom is testifying to the truth so that all those who are of the truth may hear his voice and enter into and abide in relationship with him (v. 37). He gives the gift of truth by giving himself both in his revelatory dialogues with those he encounters and in the giving of his life. According to the Prologue, those who receive him (who are of the truth) are empowered to become children of God (1:12). The narrator later clarifies that Jesus will further lay down his life to draw into one the scattered children of God (11:51–52). The imagery that accompanies Jesus' offer of relationship in truth and the language used in narration and direct speech is the language of covenant. This self-revelation of Jesus to Pilate and the implicit gift of truth that accompanies it constitute an offer of covenant to Pilate. Pilate has come in to question Jesus openly and, as he does in every dialogue across the Gospel, Jesus engages Pilate in a dialogue in which he offers himself as the gift of truth. By responding to Jesus the way Pilate does, with the brusque rhetorical question, "What is truth?" followed by an immediate exit (18:38), Pilate dismisses Jesus' challenge. Further, he shows that he does not really understand the question, that is, the truth of relationship in covenant with God that is at stake. By not being open to the revelation of Jesus and the offer of truth, Pilate fails to recognize the gift of truth that is standing in front of him. Therefore his attempts to remain neutral, to act as if the person and fate of Jesus have nothing to do with him, also fail (18:38b—19:8). Eventually even his appeals to his own power before Jesus, and his attempts to act decisively before "the Jews" fail as well (19:9–15).

The sheep that are of Jesus' fold hear his voice of truth and enter into abiding covenantal relationship with him as empowered children of God. There are others who, when challenged by Jesus' revelation of this gift of truth, not only reject the offer of relationship in covenant, but also use all human means to rid themselves of the perceived threat his person and offer constitute.

In the Fourth Gospel, "the Jews" represent this group who oppose Jesus, and their rejection reaches its climax here at the Roman trial. Pilate, then, constitutes a third possible response to Jesus as the questioner who is given the revelation of truth and the challenge to accept the relationship as a child of God that Jesus' offers. In the end, he proves himself to be so committed to human endeavor and the powers of this world (including his own) that he cannot understand what is really being asked of him. He fails to see the truth when it is standing before him and thus, despite all efforts to exert his own will, hands the Truth over to its enemies to be crucified. Nonetheless, the gift of truth that God has offered through Jesus does not come to an end with his earthly life and mission. Human response and failure cannot thwart God's plan and cannot negate God's covenantal action in the world. Indeed, the full glorification of the Son is perfected by his being lifted up on the cross. It is then that his mission is perfected and he can say, "It is finished" (19:30), and "gather into one the scattered children of God" (11:52).

THE CRUCIFIXION OF JESUS BEFORE THE JEWS—COMPLETION (19:16B–37)

The act of the crucifixion of Jesus is presented in five scenes, framed by introductory verses of character and setting (19:16b–18) and concluding verses of reflection upon the consequences of the action (19:35–37). The central scenes narrate the inscription, the seamless tunic, Jesus' interaction with his mother and the Beloved Disciple, Jesus' last words, and the piercing of Jesus' side (vv. 19–34). In a moment of profound dramatic irony, Jesus' last breaths on the cross establish the church, symbolized by the garment that cannot be torn apart. The Beloved Disciple and the mother come together "because of that hour" (v. 27). The earthly life and ministry of the Son of Man culminates in the affirmation that all has been brought to perfection (vv. 28–30). The intensifying fulfillment language across the passion narrative comes to its climax here as the Beloved Disciple, now given into the family of the new community of God, affirms the truth of his testimony so that all future audiences may believe that these things took place that the Scripture might be fulfilled (vv. 35–36). The new community of the children of God immediately begins its own mission of faith and witness through the testimony of the Beloved Disciple who is joined in the community of family with the mother of Jesus.

Jesus Is Buried by His Friends in a Garden (19:38–42)

The passion narrative is brought full circle as Jesus comes once again into a garden, this time brought to rest in a new tomb by friends (vv. 40–42). Nicodemus finishes his journey as he comes forward with spices to anoint Jesus for his burial (v. 39). Joseph of Arimathea fulfills his role of providing the burial place (v. 39). The scene is set for what was destroyed in a garden (18:1; see also Gen 1—3) to be restored in a garden (John 20).

The Resurrection of the Word (John 20)

The postresurrection narratives begin at John 20. These episodes are broadly presented in two acts, again distinguished by geography: at the empty tomb (vv. 1–18) and in the upper room (vv. 19–29). At the tomb in the garden, the action centers first around Peter and the Beloved Disciple (vv. 1–9), then around Mary Magdalene (vv. 10–18). Mary's commission leads her to the disciples to give her message (v. 18). The action is then taken up in the disciples' room, first without the presence of Thomas (vv. 19–25), then later with Thomas in attendance (vv. 26–29). The final verses conclude both these postresurrection narratives and the body of the Gospel (vv. 30–31). These scenes present the Evangelist's story of the resurrection of the Word of God through the lens of his concern for the early Christian community of believers.

John 20 begins with Mary at the empty tomb with no concept of a resurrection (v. 1). The Beloved Disciple is the first to see the signs of death overcome and believe, but Peter's response is not recorded (v. 8). Once they depart, Mary is left again to go through her own journey of faith with Jesus, the "Gardener" (vv.

11–17). She becomes the apostle to the apostles as she fulfills the commission Jesus gives her (v. 18). Mary prepares the disciples so that when Jesus appears to them, they are overjoyed and receive both the Holy Spirit and their own commission.

The Evangelist then provides Thomas's journey of faith through Jesus' encounters with the remaining disciples (vv. 19–25, 26–29). Thomas's journey within the story comes to completion when he sees Jesus for who he is and finally believes. His exclamation provides a profession of faith for all those who have made this journey: "My Lord and my God" (v. 28). For his part, Jesus blesses the next generation of readers, who, like the Beloved Disciple, will believe without seeing. Jesus' first words to potential disciples and his first words of the Gospel: "What do you seek?" (1:38) and "Come and you will see" (1:39), are balanced by his blessing, his final words in the body of the Gospel to all disciples who live beyond his earthly ministry in his new covenantal community of believers: "Blessed are those who have not seen and yet have come to believe" (v. 29). The Book of Glory comes to an end with the closing remarks through which the author makes his claim for writing Scripture so that readers and audiences for all time might believe that Jesus is the Christ, the Son of God, and thereby might have life in his name (vv. 30–31).

Jesus and the Glory of God

The covenant imagery in this second half of the Gospel is subtle, though extensive and complex. The Evangelist continues to weave the language and symbolism of the OT covenant metaphor through his presentation of the good news of Jesus Christ without overtly making covenantal claims in so far as using the term itself. Rather, the Evangelist sets scenes, formulates characters, and recounts dialogue that resonate the OT covenant narratives, symbols, and themes so as to continue to present Jesus as the new covenantal gift that is also truth. In his encounters with people in John 13—20, Jesus continues to offer himself as the revelation of God and relationship with himself as an abiding relationship that constitutes the children of God.

Jesus' final meal and last discourse with his disciples is recounted in John 13—17. The action and dialogue of Jesus and his disciples narrated in those chapters reflect the covenantal renewal ceremonies of the OT, and particularly that of Joshua 24. Jesus' public ministry has come to a close. Those who received Jesus reconstitute "his own" in the world and these he will love to the end (13:1) by renewing and sealing his covenant with them as he turns toward his glorification. The evening begins with Jesus washing the feet of his disciples and sharing a meal with them. This action sets the stage for his lengthy discourse that follows the general form of covenant challenge, promises, obligations, and consequences of a covenant renewal ceremony. The disciples respond to Jesus' discourse with the affirmation that they understand and accept him, his mission, and the future mission he has laid out for them. Jesus concludes the process with a prayer on their behalf that seals their covenant. At the close of his final words of prayer, Jesus' passion begins.

Everything that happens in John 18—19 first moves Jesus and those around him to the cross then emanates from Jesus' lifting up in glory. The covenantal aspect of the dialogues of the Roman trial focus primarily upon the question of truth, and the correlating question of kingship and the nature of the kingdom of Jesus. Although Jesus is fully in control of his destiny throughout the passion account, and certainly through this proceeding, it is Pilate and his vigorous movement between the truth of Jesus and security of the world that structures the dialogue. Jesus extends the challenge of covenant to Pilate through the revelation of himself and his kingship as the gift of truth. Pilate's dismissive response "What is truth?" proves that not only does he not understand the fullness of the revelation that stands before him, but furthermore, he cannot endeavor beyond the human realm of political maneuvering and status-seeking. From this point forward, regardless of Pilate's efforts he is powerless to effect any real decision. Ultimately, as Jesus has foretold, Pilate hands Jesus over to be crucified, and the lifting up is accomplished (19:16–37; see 8:28; 12:32–33).

The crucifixion proceeds swiftly and Jesus dies with the inscription "The King of the Jews" placed above him (19:19–21).

In his final moments, Jesus gazes upon his mother at the foot of the cross (19:26). Jesus' mother, the first to believe and to begin to live in covenant relationship with him (2:1–12), and the disciple whom Jesus loved stand before him. Jesus gives to his mother, the model disciple before "the hour," a new son in the Beloved Disciple, the one who emerged as the model disciple during "the hour" of Jesus' glory, sealed in covenant relationship with Jesus. This disciple is introduced as "beloved" at 13:23 where he reclined on the lap of Jesus just as Jesus reclined on the lap of the Father (1:18). He appears at all the key moments of the passion narrative and the narrator eventually affirms that, like Jesus before him, this disciple's testimony is true. He thus functions as the representative of the Johannine community. Jesus then completes the family formation by giving to the Beloved Disciple his mother in kinship. By using performative language, Jesus' pronouncement accomplishes the new relationship that it declares. By his declaration, Jesus constitutes a new family. The theological significance of "the hour" of Jesus is affirmed when the narrator explains that "because of that hour" the Beloved Disciple takes his new mother into his own. From the beginning, the Evangelist has employed the language of kinship to characterize the believer's new relationship to God, in covenant with Jesus (see 1:12; 11:52). Here at the foot of the cross, the formation of this new family is the heart of the future community of believers. The establishment of a covenantal community of family that lives beyond the earthly life of Jesus culminates in Jesus' last words, "It is finished."

The body of the Gospel then comes to a close with the postresurrection narratives that send this community forward with the memory of their encounters with Jesus, now the risen Lord (John 20). Jesus sends Mary Magdalene forth as the apostle with the message of his rising to his "brothers," the new family of his own (v. 17). The final words of direct speech of the body of the Gospel point beyond the first generation to the Johannine community and the community of readers who take the covenant of abiding in relationship with Jesus into the future, "Have you believed because you have seen me? Blessed are those who have not seen and yet have come to believe" (v. 29). With these words, the narrator can then conclude the body of the Gospel with the proclamation that this Scripture has indeed been written so that the community of readers may be affirmed in their belief and may go forward into the world of their future as the covenantal community of Christ (vv. 30–31).

Questions for Review

1. How does the second half of the body of the Gospel, the Book of Glory, relate to the first half, the Book of Signs?

2. John 13—17 is considered the "last discourse" of the Gospel and occurs between Jesus and "his own" during and after their last meal together before his arrest. What is the focus of this lengthy series of actions and dialogues?

3. How is Jesus portrayed throughout the events of the passion narrative (John 18—19)? What is the significance of the Roman trial and Pilate's query on the nature of *truth*?

4. What happens at the foot of the cross on both the narrative and covenantal levels of the Gospel? In this vein, what is the significance of Jesus' final words on the cross: "it is finished" (which could also be translated, "it is completed, or "it is perfected")?

5. In the Gospel of John, who is Nicodemus, on both the narrative and the teaching levels of the story? Why must we not overlook his story within this story of good news?

6. In the Gospel of John, who is Mary Magdalene on both the narrative and the teaching levels of the story? Why might she be so important within this story of the good news?

7. In John 20, Thomas demands to see in order to believe in the resurrection of Jesus. Why is this final scene of the Book of Glory so important for readers of the Gospel? What is the Evangelist teaching here?

5

ENDINGS AND THE PROMISE OF THE NEW COMMUNITY IN CHRIST

The body of the Gospel narrative has culminated in the glorification of Jesus Christ the Son of God. In John 1:1—20:31 the Evangelist gives a commanding and cohesive narrative to show his audience how a community is to live in covenant relationship with God through Jesus Christ. John 20:30–31 provides a powerful initial conclusion to this story. In John 21 the Evangelist provides a continuation of the community and a sign for how it is to go on in the absence of the incarnate Jesus. This epilogue provides a foundation for the church and its leadership that is not addressed in the body of the Gospel. The fishing expedition and the dialogue between Jesus, Peter, and the Beloved Disciple provide unifying models for all who believe for all time. It is to these "endings" that we now turn.

What's in an Ending?

Chapter 20 of John's Gospel begins to bring the story to a close with several accounts of appearances of the resurrected Jesus. Through his interactions with the disciples in verses 1–29, Jesus fulfills his promises to return to them (14:18–19; 16:16); and they are able to begin to understand the word of Jesus about the raising of the temple of his body (2:19–22). As the journey of the disciples begins to reach its peak, the Evangelist, as author, turns to readers and audiences of all times to bring them to the heart of their own faith decisions. Thomas's ultimate acclamation and Jesus' response, which both accepts Thomas's confession of faith and blesses those beyond the time of the Gospel who can believe without seeing, bring the story to its culmination. The vast majority of scholars thus posit John 20:30–31 as the conclusion to the body of the Gospel, with John 21 following as an epilogue. In these final verses of John 20, the Fourth Evangelist provides his storytelling strategy (choosing from many signs and traditions; v. 30) and the purpose of what he has written (encouraging belief; v. 31).

Biblical scholars then often ponder the intent—and even the existence—of chapter 21 of the Gospel according to John given the concluding sounds of 20:30–31. Nonetheless, no ancient manuscript exists without the scenes of this chapter as the final act of the Gospel. Many of these same scholars also agree that the Gospel was likely composed in stages over a period of time. This final chapter was probably added late in the composition history of the Gospel to respond to the changing needs and circumstances of the Johannine community. John 21 therefore can be understood as an epilogue insofar as it brings the Gospel story beyond its conclusion into the time of its early audience and clarifies the form and mission of the community it engenders. An epilogue, as an "afterword," *carries forward* some aspect of the narrative by describing the consequences resulting from its climax, its solution or outcome. This epilogue is best contextualized in terms of the problems emerging in the community as reflected in the Johannine Letters that will be the focus of the next chapter. Broadly speaking, the covenant relationship made possible by Jesus in the Gospel of John leaves its community with only two commands: *to love* and *to believe* (see 12:36; 13:19, 34–35; 14:1, 11, 15, 21, 23, 24; 15:9–10, 12, 13, 17). However completely these truths are revealed, living through them as a community can become problematic over time when members differ on who and what exactly to love and to believe. The resulting issues can be summarized as an ecclesial problem: the question of who we are to "love" and incorporate into our understanding of church; and an authority problem: the question of what we are to believe and whose lead we are to follow in determining doctrine. The former is handled in the first part of John 21 (vv. 1–14), and the latter in the second part (vv. 15–23). The final two verses (vv. 24–25) offer a second conclusion that sends the audience out into the world beyond the Gospel.

The following pages will offer brief analyses of these conclusions to the Gospel of John, with more attention given to the epilogue. Focus will naturally rest on the light these final scenes shed on the underlying covenant theme of the Gospel.

The Conclusion (John 20:30–31)

> Now Jesus did many other signs in the presence of his disciples that are not written in this book. But these are written that you may go on believing that Jesus is the Messiah, the Son of God, and that through believing you may have life in his name.

In the final verses of the body of his account, the narrator shares with the audience that the chronicle of who Jesus is was not exhausted by his story. Rather, the Evangelist has chosen from the wealth of traditions about Jesus in crafting his narrative. Here he uses his preferred term for Jesus' miraculous activity, *sēmeia*, "signs." The choice of this term is particularly pointed for the signifying role this activity carries throughout the Gospel. The term also resonates with the Evangelist's intended audience as it recalls the "signs" of Moses on behalf of God during the Exodus narrative (Exod 4:8, 9, 17, 28, 30; 7:3; 10:1, 2), as well as God's own action to signify his glory in the Sinai wilderness (Num 14:11, 22; Deut 4:34; 6:22; 7:19; 11:3; 16:38; 26:8; 29:3; 31:13, 17; 34:11). In verse 31, he asserts that this was done not only for literary purposes—to shape a compelling story, but also for theological purposes—to reveal God's action. He affirms his purpose in terms of what "is written" to indicate his understanding of his Gospel narrative as providing his audience both binding commands and prophecy fulfillment as part of, and quite possibly the goal of, the Scripture—the story of God's action in the world. There is a notable textual difficulty here in verse 31. Early manuscripts attest two different grammatical forms of the verb "to believe." Some ancient manuscripts use the form of the verb which could be translated, "that you may come to believe" (called the aorist subjunctive in Greek). This would indicate that the Evangelist's intended audience was receiving this good news for the first time and his purpose is to bring about belief. Other ancient manuscripts use the form of the verb which could be translated, "that you may continue believing" (called the present subjunctive in Greek). The translation provided above opts for the latter, the interpretive force of which is that the Evangelist is writing to a community of believers who are making their own journeys of faith, which include facing doubt, opposition, and rejection, so that they "may go on believing." He wants to affirm that they, and any audience, have chosen the right path and to encourage them to hold fast. The second clause of the verse provides both the content ("that Jesus is the Christ, the Son of God") and the result ("life in his name") of that ongoing action of believing. Regardless of any mainstream social, cultural, and theological categories of the world that may reject them, the Johannine community of readers and listeners have chosen the path that fulfills Scripture and gives the true gift of life as children of God.

The Epilogue (John 21)

Regardless of how potent the final words of John 20 are, or what a strong conclusion to the narrative they might be, the Gospel has one more story to tell. The intricacy of the account of John 21 is revealed in the introduction of the primary characters of the second scene in the setting and action of the first scene. Jesus manifested himself one final time to the disciples (v. 1). The audience can interpret the story as a theophany, or manifestation of God's presence among the disciples. In this final postresurrection encounter, Jesus sends his community of disciples out into the world as leaders of and witnesses to the new covenant community. By closing his story with this epilogue, the Evangelist simultaneously answers questions developing in his own community of believers regarding the church and its authority by reconciling and resolving the respective roles of Peter and the Beloved Disciple in the journey of faith.

The encounter by the Sea of Tiberias (another name for the Sea of Galilee) is introduced as occurring sometime after the events of John 20 ("After these things..."; v. 1). Seven of Jesus' disciples are identified and gathered by the sea. They go out fishing following the lead of Peter (vv. 2–3). Readers should be alerted by Peter's announcement of his intent to fish. Should Peter be spending his time in such a way at this point in the narrative? Is he returning to his old occupation? Or is this night of fishing just a harmless and temporary diversion? We must remember that Peter last appeared as an active participant in the Gospel warming himself by a charcoal fire with the enemies of Jesus in the court of the high priest (18:18, 25–27). There Peter denied Jesus three times as Jesus predicted he would (18:18, 25, 27; see 13:38). Peter had sworn that he would lay down his life for Jesus (13:37), but Jesus prevented him from doing so when Peter tried to defend him in the garden (18:10–11). Peter, the earnest, aggressive spokesman for the disciples (see 6:68–69; 13:6–10, 24, 36–37; 18:10–11) was thrown from his former self-understanding and found himself denying all knowledge of and relationship with Jesus (18:18–27). In John 20, Peter appeared at the empty tomb at Mary Magdalene's behest, but had no dialogue. Indeed, unlike the Beloved Disciple who saw and believed, readers are given no insight into Peter's state of mind or faith (20:2–10). In the present scene, then, we can see that Peter has returned to the occupation of fishing, the covenant relationship he accepted from Jesus broken. A primary focus of the remainder of the chapter is therefore to reconstitute the covenant relationship between Jesus and Peter and set Peter in his role of pastoral authority over the community of Jesus' flock (21:1, 15–19; see 10:1–16). Before that happens, the nature of the ecclesial community is affirmed.

After a long night of failure, morning breaks to reveal Jesus standing on the shore. He greets his disciples by addressing them as "children" (v. 5). These are the same sentiments for the disciples expressed in the covenant renewal of the last discourse where the disciples were characterized as "his own" (13:1) and Jesus called them "children" (13:33). This greeting of Jesus for his disciples recalls the identity of the covenant community as "children of God" (1:12; 11:52) and sets the stage for the wondrous catch and renewal to come (vv. 6-11, 15-17). The Beloved Disciple, in keeping with his character established in chapters 13—20 as the one who witnesses and gives access to the other disciples, is the first to recognize Jesus: "It is the Lord!" (v. 7). Peter, also in keeping with the earnest zeal of his character, wraps himself in his garment and jumps into the sea in an effort to get to Jesus (v. 7). As they all reach the land, Peter returns to the boat on Jesus' command to haul ashore the wondrous catch of fish in the unbroken net. Many interpreters, both ancient and contemporary, have tried to assign a specific meaning to the total catch at 153 fish. The abundance of fish reminds the reader of the abundance of wine (2:1-12) and the abundance of food (6:1-14) provided by Jesus, and indicates the fullness and inclusivity of the church. Drawing from the OT prophets, this abundance motif underlines the presence of the messianic era (see Hos 2:19-20; Isa 25:6-8; Jer 2:2). The universal character of the mission of the community consists of bringing into one the children of God scattered over the earth (see 11:52). The unbroken net reflects the unity of the community in the new life given by Jesus. By facilitating this miraculous and somehow perfectly complete catch when all hope appeared to be lost, the risen Jesus, the giver of new life and the power to become children of God, signals the actualization of the new covenant community. If the question is, "Who are we to love?" The answer is, "Everyone!" This new covenant community is universal, open to all who receive and believe that Jesus is the Christ.

The ecclesial issue at stake is thus addressed by the sign Jesus performs for the disciples signifying the universal nature of the church and its mission. The second part of John 21 properly situates authority in this inclusive church (vv. 15-23). Peter is designated the leader, the head of the church; the Beloved Disciple is the witness, and the ideal model disciple in the church. Jesus has brought Peter and the disciples around a new charcoal fire and provided a meal of bread and fish (vv. 9-13). The charcoal fire is a narrative marker that calls to mind Peter's last scene of covenant breach with Jesus. This meal recalls their final meal together before Jesus' passion as well as the miraculous feeding and the ritual covenant meals of the OT (see John 6:1–15; 13:1–11; Gen 26:26–30; 31:43–54; Exod 24:5–11; Deut 27:6–7). Although all seven disciples are involved in the meal and its aftermath, the narrative has placed a steady focus on Peter (vv. 3, 7, 11), and the reconciliation of Peter's relationship with Jesus will take center stage in the following verses (vv. 15–22). Jesus confronts Peter at every step, challenging his upset equilibrium and pushing him toward a difficult reconciliation that will allow Peter to take action in a new role.

In this context of a covenant meal, Jesus asks Peter three times if he loves him (vv. 15, 16, 17), reconstituting Peter's three-time denial into a binding relationship with the consequences of mission and leadership. Jesus initiates the dialogue with the comparative "more than these" (v. 15), a phrase that is difficult to interpret. What or who are "these"? Understanding Jesus' question of Peter's love for him as a comparison to Peter's love for other things calls to mind the absolute claim for love and commitment that God makes on those who enter into covenant, which is set over and against everything else (see especially Deut 6:5; 7:9; 10:12; 11:1; 13:3; 30:36; Josh 22:5). This scene began with Peter returning to what could be characterized as the comfort of his former way of life, especially given the state of his current self-understanding. Jesus' question is best understood as a challenge to Peter to let go of his old life and his old self once and for all and re-enter into life in Jesus' name. This is a difficult process for Peter. He is anguished by the third repetition of the question and humbled by the insight and knowledge of Jesus. Jesus does, however, make the move toward Peter, approaching and accepting him where he is. Jesus' threefold question and Peter's threefold response reconciles their breached relationship and renews the covenant between them—all based in love. Jesus' commands that follow from this renewed covenant articulate Peter's mission as action in service of the new covenant community. He is to "feed" and "tend" the flock (vv. 15, 16, 17). Peter's leadership is clarified pastorally as he is mandated as the shepherd of the burgeoning flock of the children of God. Peter's journey then comes to an end as Jesus demands his obedience and implicates his eventual crucifixion in parallel to Jesus' own: "Follow me" (vv. 19, 22).

Then what of the Beloved Disciple? The Evangelist must speak to the destiny and mortality of the disciple whom Jesus loved who has journeyed and abided with Jesus throughout the Gospel story. The narrator closes by describing the unique mandate of the Beloved Disciple (vv. 21–24). He would not die a martyr's death, but live a long life as the true disciple and witness. When Peter asks about the Beloved Disciple's fate, Jesus focuses his attention on his own faithfulness and role in the new covenant relationship. Already in the first century of the church, there is a concern for the recognition of the pastoral role of authority and the testimonial role of discipleship. These roles can, but do not have to be incorporated in one person. The best disciple is not necessarily the shepherd of the community, and the best leader is not necessarily a model disciple. Therefore, in this Gospel these roles are embodied in two separate characters, Peter and the Beloved Disciple. If the question is, "Who is our leader and authority?" The answer is, "Peter!" The Johannine community is to remain in union with the developing church under the leadership and authority of Peter. But if the question is, "Who is our witness and model for discipleship?" The answer is, "The Beloved Disciple." He is the treasured founder of the community and his eye-witness testimony is the heart of their bond and ongoing existence.

The narrator then concludes his story by attesting to its limitless nature (v. 25). He speaks in the first person and sends his readers and listeners into the world and their shared future as the new covenant community of God, as children living in the love and faith of Jesus.

The Promise of the New Community of Christ

The first conclusion to the body of the Gospel of John opens the door for its readers to situate themselves as the disciples of Jesus whose belief is affirmed and reaffirmed as they journey through "life in his name" (20:31). In her work on the endings of the Gospels, biblical scholar Morna Hooker says of the Fourth Gospel, "The book may have come to a tidy end, but John does not expect us to put the book back on our shelves with a sigh of satisfaction and the thought that this was a good story: this is meant to be the kind of book that changes lives."[1] The epilogue, John 21, is a portrait of how that can happen. Every disciple has a role in the new covenant community and should seek to understand and nurture that role with single-minded faithfulness. It is not one's concern what Jesus has in store for another; rather each person's call is to strive to live life in his name, cherishing and fostering whatever form that may take. This, in turn, becomes the uniting force of the new covenant community.

Questions for Review

1. How does the blessedness of believing without seeing—that is, believing in the word of Jesus—bring unity to both the Gospel story and the Gospel's community of believers?
2. Why is it helpful to consider John 21 as an epilogue to the body of the Gospel narrative?
3. How does John 21 help the new covenant community in its ongoing relationships both within the Johannine community and with those across the developing church?

---

1. Hooker, *Endings*, 74.

6

COVENANT AND COMMUNITY IN THE LETTERS OF JOHN

We can now study the Letters of John as the canonical extension of the community of the Gospel and the challenges it faced as Christianity grew and developed in an ever-changing world toward the end of the first century AD. We discuss them last because the Letters of John are among the latest documents of the NT. In addition, it is largely through the association of 1 John with the Fourth Gospel that the latter gained its place in the NT canon. We will therefore begin by discussing the background of the Johannine Epistles in terms of their placement in the NT, and then turn our attention to the covenant theme as it continues to weave through the fabric of these later literary expressions of the community of the Beloved Disciple.

The Letters of John in the New Testament

As we discussed in the introduction, several documents in the NT are regarded by the Christian tradition as originating in a single person named "John." In addition to the Gospel according to John, three Letters of John and the Book of Revelation complete that tradition. Only the Book of Revelation refers to its author by the name "John," and he identifies himself as an Elder or "Presbyter" writing from the island of Patmos (Rev 1:9). No historically verifiable evidence links John the Elder at Patmos with any of the disciples, but a long tradition associates all five of these documents with the disciple of Jesus, John the Son of Zebedee. Similar to the anonymity of the Gospel, there is no address or salutation at all in 1 John. The author of 2 and 3 John describes himself as "the Elder" (v. 1 in each) but this expression was widely used in the early church, and can be found in many Christian documents. Thus, on the basis of the documents alone, it is not clear that "the Elder" of Revelation and "the Elder" of 2 and 3 John are the same, or that one person named "John" was the "Elder" John of Revelation, the "Elder" of 2 and 3 John, the author of 1 John, and the Beloved Disciple of the Gospel.

As early as AD 180, however, the church leader Irenaeus became a vital advocate of this literature and first made the link between John, the Son of Zebedee, and the Beloved Disciple. A large number of Christians had been attracted to a form of Christianity called Gnosticism that was strongly influenced by speculative Greco-Roman religions. One of Gnosticism's many features was the way in which it minimized the importance of the physical life and death of Jesus—even denying that there ever was a real human life or a real experience of death. The Gnostics were very fond of John's Gospel, which provided them with a story of Jesus that was less down to earth than that of Matthew, Mark, and Luke. Irenaeus fought hard against Gnosticism, and strove to show that the Fourth Gospel was deeply embedded in the life and death of the man, Jesus of Nazareth, and not just an extraordinary speculation. One of the major elements that enabled Irenaeus to rescue the Gospel of John for the Christian community was the identification of the author of the Letter we now call 1 John with the author of the Fourth Gospel. In that Letter, so many of the same theological, christological, and ethical issues were stated in a more grounded, "orthodox" fashion. Irenaeus went on to identify the Beloved Disciple, and thus the author of both works, as John the Son of Zebedee, one of the founding apostles of the Christian church. This position has been held down to our own time by the tradition, and, indeed, no modern scholar denies the close relationship between 1 John and the Fourth Gospel. In the early tradition, this connection was eventually extended first to what we call 2 John, then also to 3 John. The similarity of the message and the repetition of the title "the Elder" in both Letters led the church fathers eventually to regard 1, 2, and

3 John as the Johannine Letters, and as part of the NT canon along-side the Gospel.

The Emergence of the Covenant Metaphor

Through his pioneering work in the 1970s entitled *Interiority and Covenant*, Edward Malatesta raised the question of covenant in the Johannine literature by studying the syntactic use of the verbal constructions "to be in" and "to abide in" in the First Letter of John.[1] In this study, he focuses on what he calls "interiority expressions" of being and abiding (the latter sometimes translated "remaining") in God through Christ and their resonance of the OT new covenant themes expressed particularly in the prophets Jeremiah and Ezekiel. Beginning with covenant formulas in the OT, he focuses on the concept of the divine indwelling. What comes to the fore in this study is the explicit interior renewal aspect of the new covenant texts in Jeremiah and Ezekiel. While the Jeremiah texts manifest "an interiorization of the Law, knowledge of God, and forgiveness of sins," the Ezekiel texts reveal God's promises of "another heart and a new spirit." Malatesta concludes that the major OT themes related to covenant, and particularly to the interiorization of the new covenant are: (1) the heart, (2) the Spirit as related to indwelling, (3) the union of knowledge and justice, and (4) observance of the commandments. Once he turns his attention to the Johannine literature, Malatesta finds these interiority expressions throughout the literature but concentrated in the last discourse of the Gospel (John 13—17) and 1 John. In the end, Malatesta claims the chief characteristic of the Johannine understanding of Christianity is the awareness that the intimate relationship between Jesus, the Father, and the Spirit in turn establishes, maintains, and develops the communion of the members with God. Moreover, the communion of Christians with one another and their relationship to the world are grounded in their communion with God. From this vantage point, he further asserts that the preposition "in" is the element that converts both verbs into words

---

1. Edward Malatesta, *Interiority and Covenant: A Study of* εἶναι ἐν *and* μένειν ἐν in the First Letter of Saint John. AnBib 69 (Rome: Biblical Institute Press, 1978).

describing an interior manner of being and abiding and makes both expressions relational and therefore covenantal. Indeed, he claims that these expressions highlight the ongoing notion of the glorified Jesus as being and abiding in his disciples through the new covenant community across the generations. In sum, he asserts:

> John thus portrays for us the ideal image of the Christian community in this world, a community of human persons united with one another because [they are] united with the Father, Jesus and the Spirit. John teaches us that Christian interiority and Christian community are complementary and inseparable dimensions of life according to the New Covenant.[2]

In homage to Edward Malatesta's pioneering work in the Johannine literature, our literary overview of the covenant theme in the Letters will largely follow his lead. In addition, Raymond Brown's work in *The Community of the Beloved Disciple* continues to be foundational for the theological and historical setting of the Letters.[3] My own perception of Jesus as the new gift of truth that empowers all those who receive and believe in him to become children of God will come to the fore in terms of the community's ongoing struggle to dwell as a family in the knowledge and presence of God in a larger world that does not understand it.

The New Covenant Community

A determining factor for interpreting the three Letters of John is their historical relationship to the Gospel of John and the community that produced it. Scholars take various positions in this regard in terms of whether the Letters come from the same hand as the Gospel and whether they were written before or after the work of the Fourth Evangelist. The Gospel itself possibly underwent sev-

---

2. Malatesta, *Interiority and Covenant*, 324.

3. Raymond E. Brown, *The Community of the Beloved Disciple: The Life, Loves and Hates of an Individual Church in New Testament Times* (New York: Paulist Press, 1979).

eral drafts and refinements over the years until it reached its final form that has been preserved in the NT. It is truly the product of a community's experience of God's covenantal activity in the world. Therefore, even if the Letters did not come from the same first hand as the Gospel, they certainly arose from the same community of believers and reflect the ongoing life of that community as it seeks to come to terms with its particular understanding of the good news of Christ and God's new covenant in a world that does not receive it. Indeed, the content of the Letters is best understood as arising from the community after the crisis that lies behind the Gospel expands and extends into the community itself. If the Gospel were written c. AD 90 in a community that is defining itself over and against the rest of the world, including the mainstream Judaism of its past, then the Letters were written later in the decade at the end of the first century in a community of churches that now finds it necessary to define itself against schism from within. The ideals of the new covenant community are proving difficult to live out in a fallen world. The author writes from a position of authority to stem the tide of discord and dissolution in a possibly last-ditch effort to strengthen and unify his people.

THE FIRST LETTER OF JOHN

The relationship between 1 John and the Gospel of John becomes evident even across the first verses of the Letter. The author uses the same language and imagery in this more grounded and direct plea for the community. The covenantal language of love, knowledge, and the gift of truth for the children of God continues to permeate its pages. The prologue of the epistle mirrors the Prologue of the Gospel; and the final verses likewise echo the concluding sounds of the Gospel. Within this theological frame, the author makes three resounding appeals to the new covenant community in terms of the characteristics of God that form the heart and soul of God's children: light, justice, and love. The content of these appeals warns the community of the dangers of the world while instructing it on the power of faith to conquer all for those who abide in Christ and thus remain in the new covenant community. The Letter could thus be outlined as follows:

1 John

1:1–4 Prologue: The Word of Life for the Community
1:5—2:28 Opening Appeal to the New Covenant Community:
  God Is Light
    1:5—2:2 The Experience of the Light: The Word of God in
    Jesus
    2:3–11 The Message of the Light: Knowledge of God Is
    Fellowship in God
    2:12–27 The Crisis of the Light: The Dangers of the World
2:28—4:6 Central Appeal to the New Covenant Community:
  God Is Just
    2:28—3:10 The Mark of the True Children of God
    3:11–24 The New Covenant Commandment
    4:1–6 Discernment and the Testing of Spirits
4:7—5:12 Closing Appeal to the New Covenant Community:
  God Is Love
    4:7–21 The Presence of God in Relationship: Love for God
    and One Another
    5:1–12 The Foundation of Love: Faith that Conquers the
    World
5:13–21 Epilogue: Prayer for the Faithful Community

The author states his purpose in the prologue with intentional echoes of both Genesis and the new "beginning" of the Gospel Prologue (John 1:1–18). But "the word of life" he declares is only that which the community has collectively perceived through the senses—what they have "heard," "seen," "looked at," and "touched" (v. 1). Therefore he can "testify" to that which has been "revealed" (v. 2). This is the mark of the true fellowship he wishes for the community grounded in the complete joy of union with God the Father and Jesus Christ the Son (v. 3). The ensuing appeals are all written toward this goal.

The opening appeal is the proclamation that God is Light in terms of the community's experience of the Light (1:5—2:2), the message of the Light itself (2:3–11), and the crisis the Light faces in this world (2:12–27). Based on their own experience of the Light, the community is called to acknowledge the Word of God in Jesus. Here the author gives insight into the conflict that has arisen in the community. In a series of conditional statements, he asserts that the claim to be without sin lies outside of the truth. To claim such is to make a liar of Jesus and his blood that cleanses this sin. Furthermore, just as Jesus spoke of the Holy Spirit as the Advocate for humankind in the last discourse (John 13—17), the author speaks of Jesus as the Advocate for humankind and its sinful nature before the Father. Indeed, the indwelling of the Word in truth leads to the covenantal assertion that Jesus "is the atoning sacrifice for our sins, and not for ours only but also for the sins of the whole world" (2:2). This experience is affirmed in the Light's central message that knowledge of God leads to fellowship in God. The core of this appeal is replete with the covenantal language of obedience and knowledge of God that are themselves affirmed by keeping the new covenant commandments of believing in Christ and loving one another. This is how the community will abide in the Light. The language of family returns in the final section of this first appeal as the author warns of the dangers of the world. As he did in 2:1, he again echoes the covenantal call of the Gospel to be "children of God" (John 1:12; 11:52) as he warns them against those who "went out from us" (2:18–19). Here we have the strongest indication of the fragmentation the community is experiencing. Those who left are somehow denying that Jesus is the Christ, rendering them antichrists. By contrast, knowledge of the truth of Christ will keep the children safe. This leads to the heart of the first appeal: "Let what you heard from the beginning abide in you...then you will abide in the Son and in the Father" (2:24).

The central appeal to the new covenant community emphasizes that God is Just in terms of the mark of the true children of God (2:28—3:10), who are known by their keeping of the new covenant commandment (3:11–24) and their ability to discern and test spirits (4:1–6). The justice, or righteousness, of God will manifest in the children of God as a strong sense of ethics. Indeed the hope of the children of God is union with God in his image and likeness. This ethic is once again based in the commandments of the new covenant to believe in the name Jesus Christ and to love one another—and be known by this way of life (3:23). This abiding reality is expressed in the heart of this central appeal, "Little children, let us love, not in word or speech, but in truth and action" (3:18). Abiding by this ethic brings the Spirit of God into the fellowship of the community and both empowers and emboldens the community to stand fast against the spirit of the world. The author can thus conclude this appeal with the consoling security of covenant: "Little children, you are from God, and have conquered them; for the one who is in you is greater than the one who is in the world" (4:4).

The author's closing appeal to his new covenant community focuses on the attribute of God that embodies all other characteristics—that God is Love. This is revealed in their love for one another when God is present in their relationships with each other and with God (4:7–21), as well as in the foundation of all love: a faith that conquers the world (5:1–12). Indeed, he begins his final appeal with the imperative for his "beloved": "Let us love one another, because love is from God." The author follows this command with his characteristic formulation of the new covenant of the children of God: "Everyone who loves is born of God and knows God" (4:7). God's love is witnessed by the gift of the atoning sacrifice of his Son and is perfected in the ongoing mutual indwelling love of the community. The language of being and abiding in God and love comes to the fore in these verses as he demands the presence of God in their relationships. The heart of this closing appeal is, therefore, "The commandment we have from him is this: those who love God must love their brothers and sisters also" (4:21). The result of this love is the victory of faith, and this faith conquers the world (5:4–5). The author has already affirmed the atoning sacrifice of Christ, now he upholds the incarnation of Jesus as God's testimony through the Spirit of truth that the one who believes that Jesus is the Son of God has life, and this life in faith conquers all the dangers of this world (5:6–12).

Echoing John 20:30–31, 1 John concludes with a purpose statement through which the author shares his desire for the children of God to go on believing in the name of the Son of God, and thereby have knowledge of eternal life (5:13–21). He affirms their boldness in prayer as fundamental communication in this relationship, for "we know that we are God's children" (v. 19). The covenantal language of the Letter culminates in the closing thoughts of the epilogue:

And we know that the Son of God has come and has given us understanding so that we may know him who is true; and we are in him who is true, in his Son Jesus Christ. He is the true God and eternal life. (1 John 5:20)

THE SECOND AND THIRD LETTERS OF JOHN

The brevity of the final two epistles neither mitigates their power nor the insight they give into the challenges faced by this early Christian community that would have appealed to accept all humankind in covenant. By this stage the faithful are struggling and the community is falling prey to the contentiousness of human nature and the pressures of the larger world. The two Letters offer direct appeals. Second John counsels a particular church within the larger Johannine community to remain in the Gospel commandment of love and to guard against deceivers. Third John offers specific praise for the fidelity of Gaius and Demetrius while warning against the betrayal of Diotrephes. The Elder thus makes his final pleas for fellowship in truth. The Letters can be outlined as follows:

2 John

> vv. 1–3 The Elder's Address to the Church: Life Lived Walking in the Truth
> vv. 4–6 Love Is the Fulfillment of the Gospel Commandment
> vv. 7–11 Believers Are to Guard against Deceivers of the Gospel
> vv. 12–13 Farewell: Appeal to Joy as the Mark of Fellowship

3 John

> vv. 1–4 The Elder's Address to Gaius: Encouragement in Love and Truth
> vv. 5–8 Praise for Hospitality—Gaius
> vv. 9–10 The Politics of Ecclesial Power—Diotrephes
> vv. 11–12 Faithfulness to the Community—Demetrius
> vv. 13–15 Farewell: Desire for Fellowship and Appeal to Friendship

The Second Letter of John is addressed to "the elect lady and her children," likely a metaphor for one of the local house churches within the extended Johannine community. The use of "children" once again denotes the new covenant family. These churches could have been some distance from each other and communication would have been maintained through letters delivered by personal couriers. In the address the Elder affirms his love for this sister church in the new gift of truth that is Jesus Christ the Father's Son who abides in them both (vv. 1–3). In the body of the Letter, he first appeals to the church to continue to keep the commandment of the new covenant and love one another (vv. 4–6), then warns her to guard against those who have split with the larger community (vv. 7–11). The Elder has rejoiced to learn that these fellow children of God are walking in truth and sharing in the love of the covenant. He seems to hope that this affirmation and appeal to continue in love will buttress them against those he calls "deceivers," who apparently not only broke with the community but seem to be actively spreading their alternative theological teaching. The one indication that the Elder gives of the content of this theology is that the deceivers "do not acknowledge Jesus Christ as coming in the flesh" (v. 7). As previously discussed, the notion that Jesus as Christ was not really human developed into the form of sectarian Christianity known as Gnosticism, which was popular in the second century AD. These beliefs have already fractured the Johannine community, and the Elder hopes to stop the spread before this sister church falls prey as well. He counsels her to abide in the Johannine teaching of the incarnation that she has heard from the beginning and thereby abide in the covenant of Christ (v. 9). The children of God are to receive and believe in Christ (John 1:12), they are not to receive these deceivers (v. 10). The unity and foundation of the covenant is at stake. The Elder closes with hopes of a future visit to continue the conversation and solidify their relationship as children of elect sisters (v. 13).

The Third Letter of John is addressed to Gaius, a Christian who is otherwise unknown in the NT literature. These Letters have been addressed increasingly more specifically, such that this third Letter is essentially a personal note indicating the splintering of the community and a final appeal to covenantal unity from the Elder to a trusted friend. He praises the prospering of Gaius's soul as he walks in truth, thereby indicating that Gaius is abiding in the covenant commandments of love and belief in the incarnate Christ. This faithfulness has brought joy and encouragement to the Elder (vv. 1–4). In the body of the Letter, he first gives attention to the reflection of truth in hospitality that has characterized Gaius's leadership (vv. 5–8), and then turns to the politics of ecclesial power in terms of a warning against Diotrephes, who does not seem to accept the Elder's authority (vv. 9–10). Here the theological disputes of the previous Letters have deteriorated into more personal conflicts with hints of factions, a decided lack of hospitality, and even expulsions from the community. The hopes for a universal egalitarian covenant community based in love and belief seem to be fading in the wake of the contentiousness of human nature. This brief Letter begins to close with a commendation of Demetrius, who may well be the letter carrier and who has proven to be one who walks in truth and faithfulness to the community (vv. 11–12). As in 2 John, the Elder closes with a desire for a personal visit to continue the conversation. He offers a final greeting to Gaius as a "friend" instead of his more typical "child." This could indicate, in keeping with John 15:12–17, where Jesus begins to call his disciples "friends" as new leaders who keep the new covenant commandments, that Gaius is a faithful fellow leader of the community who is striving for the unity for which the Elder hopes. The Elder closes his testimony of the truth and, indeed, the entirety of his correspondence preserved in the NT, with a final appeal for peace (v. 15).

The Challenge of Covenant in Community

The three Letters of John give testament both to the powerful self-giving love of God through Christ in covenant relationship with humankind, as well as to the profound frailty of the nature of that very humankind. The egalitarian call for a new covenant community to live in fellowship through believing in Jesus as the Christ and Son of God and love of both God and one another is a vocation upon which every Christian can agree. While this call to covenant relationship is never in question, the ability of humankind to live in this ideal, if unstructured, relationship in an imperfect world is. This is the challenge of covenant in community. The preservation of these Letters alongside the Gospel of John in the Sacred Scripture of Christianity gives voice to the beauty of God's love and the fire of conviction that love sparks in humankind. Jesus, John the Baptist, and the disciples of every sort, including the Elder, speak to that truth. But these works also reveal the journeys of faith and sometimes failure human beings are destined to travel in this world. The Letters indicate the beginnings of the tragic collapse of the Johannine community, but this is not the end of their story. This literature also teaches that God and God's plan succeeds even when humans fail. These Christians are integrated into the larger burgeoning faith, and their writings continue to give witness to the new covenant in Christ to which all are called. Believing and loving indeed give life in his name.

Questions for Review

1. What are the similarities among these three Letters? Note also how the Letters are addressed, how the author characterizes himself, and what the occasion of each Letter seems to be (that is, what situation or events prompted it based on what issues the writer discusses).
2. What characteristics of the author's opponents can be reconstructed from these three epistles?
3. Can you get a sense of the flow of thought of this correspondence? If you had to articulate themes for each Letter, what would they be?
4. How might you characterize the distinctive themes shared by the Gospel and Letters of John?
5. How might the Letters shed light on the Gospel and/or on the community of the Evangelist?
6. What might be important about the inclusion of this common literature in the NT canon?

CONCLUSION

COVENANT AND THE COMMUNITY OF THE BELOVED DISCIPLE

In these concluding pages, we will bring together the force of the literary and theological theme of covenant in the Gospel and Letters of John. We can then speculate on the meaning of living in covenant relationship for the first-century community of the Beloved Disciple that speaks to audiences of the Johannine literature for all time.

Covenant: God's Promise

One of my favorite quotes about the Gospel of John comes from the introduction to Charles Giblin's work on John's passion narrative, where he claims that "as every Irishman knows, the meaning of a story lies largely in the way it is told. For each storyteller wants himself to be understood appreciatively through his own way of telling the tale, whether that tale is not as yet known or, and indeed preferably, if it already is. That is how the storyteller functions as a teacher."[1] Giblin's assertion is more pertinent for the Gospel of John than for the other canonical Gospels, and possibly more than for any other narrative in biblical literature.

---

1. Charles H. Giblin, "Confrontations in John 18, 1—27," *Bib* 65 (1984): 215.

The Fourth Evangelist is the consummate storyteller, and his distinctive style has captivated readers and writers since his version of the good news of Jesus Christ first circulated. Therefore, to attempt to gauge the impact of this Gospel and the storytelling techniques of its author, we can begin with the basic fact that the Evangelist chose to crystallize his experience of and instruction on the good news as a story. Narratives can be used to do a number of things, but one thing that narratives can do well is to draw their audiences into their worlds so as to strengthen shared values or to challenge imaginations, views, thoughts, and practices. The Fourth Evangelist composes his story of the gospel from his received traditions in his unique manner by using all the storytelling techniques at his disposal to build and bond his community. In this way he also shapes his audience's self-understanding, mission, and practice as the true children of God living in covenant relationship through the gift of truth, which is life in the name of Jesus.

The primary manner by which the Scriptures of Israel express the relationship between God and creation, in general, and Israel, in particular, is through the metaphor of the covenant relationship. Therefore, chapter 1 focused on a literary reading of the covenantal narrative preserved in the OT. That overview concluded by articulating five fundamental characteristics of the essence of biblical covenant texts and the covenantal relationship these texts emanate: *chosenness*; the offer of *covenantal promises*; the corollary human response to these first two covenantal moves on God's part—*covenantal obedience in action; the abiding presence of God* in creation and in the lives of those who accept the covenantal offer; and the purpose of the entire activity—*the knowledge of God*. This knowledge includes understanding God's binding loyalty (in terms of steadfast covenant love) and faithfulness (in terms of truth) in kinship with his people. The flourishing of this knowledge of God made possible through the dynamic of daily living in covenantal obedience breathes life into the relationship between God and his people. Likewise, however, the failure or wearing out of this knowledge threatens the very existence of the covenantal relationship. Living in the truth of the love and knowledge of God, then, is the fundamental purpose and the overarching hope of the OT covenant relationship.

The OT covenantal texts and the celebrations that recall God's saving action in the past and render that action present in the current community provide the symbolism for ongoing use of the covenant metaphor. The themes gathered from a narrative review of the OT covenant texts provide the language to articulate this hope and its lived experience in writing. The language of knowledge, love, truth, and familial kinship in the context of Israel's Scripture is thus the language of covenant. The Fourth Evangelist wove the OT covenant metaphor through the fabric of his Gospel as a guiding storytelling motif through both symbolism and dialogue as a key component of his mission to affirm for his audience that Jesus is the Christ and Son of God, and that by believing they might have life in his name. The covenant metaphor is therefore the fundamental means by which the Evangelist can echo the word of Scripture and the Johannine community can be drawn into the sacred narrative of that Scripture.

This process is begun in the Prologue to the Gospel (1:1–18). Chapter 2 presented an analysis of the Prologue that focused on the covenantal underpinnings of this first page of the narrative. Jesus, the Word become flesh, who dwelt among his own in creation, is revealed to be the gift which is truth (v. 14) that follows and perfects the former gift (v. 16) of the law of the Sinai covenant, given through Moses (v. 17). Jesus Christ makes God known (v. 18) and all who receive him, who believe in his name, are given the power to become children of God (v. 12). In the Johannine literature, "children of God" is the operative designation of those who receive and believe in Jesus and thus of the Johannine community (1:12; 11:52; implied in 3:3, 5, 7, 8, 8:31–44; 1 John 3:1–2, 10; 4:4; 5:2, 19; 2 John 4; 3 John 4). This term also describes those who are restored to new life in the Messiah based in the covenant story of Israel. As such, the "children of God," as the objects of the empowering of the Word in 1:12 and the unification in 11:52, are the true covenant community. This language of family is an essential characterization of God's covenant people. The Fourth Evangelist writes to place his community, despite any current hardship and alienation, in the genealogy of that family tree.

The life engendered by this process is not static; it is a dynamic relationship and by no means easy to achieve. Therefore, on the model of the Abraham narrative of Genesis 12—22, the Evangelist characterizes the people in both his Gospel story and his community as walking a journey with Christ. The Beloved Disciple is the character to appear to walk in union with Jesus throughout his mission. This is why he is understood as the paradigmatic disciple. Yet he is not the only one to respond to the challenge Jesus poses, a challenge that we have argued is the challenge of living in a new covenant relationship with God through Jesus. Some people respond positively and accept the gift of truth that Jesus gives. Others are not open to God's revelation in Jesus and respond negatively—rejecting Jesus and the gift he gives. Still others are characterized as either responding ambivalently or not understanding the relationship at stake and the gift of truth manifested in Jesus.

Chapters 3 and 4 presented the body of the narrative in this light. While John the Baptist is the true witness sent from God, the mother of Jesus is the first to receive the covenantal gift and believe, as she inaugurated the public ministry of Jesus. The story of her encounter and dialogue with Jesus at the wedding feast of Cana (2:1–12) was embedded in the symbolism of Pentecost and God's covenantal gift of the Law at Sinai. Covenantal obedience in action is further portrayed as the servants participate in her faith by acting on the word of Jesus. The encounter and dialogues between Jesus and "the Jews" at the feast of Tabernacles is representative of those who ultimately reject Jesus and God's ongoing covenant relationship revealed in Jesus. The symbolism of the abiding presence of God at the feast of Tabernacles, associated with both the Sinai covenant and God's care and guidance during the wilderness experience as well as hopes for the coming of the Messiah and messianic age, serve as the backdrop for this encounter. The covenantal language that dominates the dialogues includes that of abiding with Jesus, knowledge of God, and the identity of the true children of Abraham and thereby of God. Pilate is one who, through his dialogue with Jesus at the Roman trial, represents those who do not understand the gift of truth at stake in the mission and person of Jesus. Throughout the passion narrative, the language of knowledge and truth pervades the dialogues. The question of the truth revealed in Jesus reaches its pinnacle in the dialogues between Jesus and Pilate. The story of Nicodemus that begins with his dialogue with Jesus at night in John 3 and ends in his open participation in the burial of Jesus in John 19 is representative of those whose response to Jesus is ambivalent, whose journey of faith is a lengthy process of finding their way. Interspersed across this Gospel narrative is also the story of the rest of the disciples, led by Peter, with whom the audience identifies and participates in their journey of becoming children of God in the faith, knowledge, and love of the truth of God's revelation in Jesus.

Chapters 5 and 6 focused on the end of the Gospel, the Letters of John, and the life of the Johannine community beyond the biblical accounts. As an epilogue, John 21 picks up the loose threads of the Gospel narrative proper and sends the community of the Beloved Disciple out into the world with both a leader (Peter) and a model disciple (the Beloved), as well as a mission (to love and follow the word of Christ) for the new covenant community. The Letters, 1, 2, and 3 John, show the beginnings of the tragic collapse of that first community. It appears that the ongoing struggle of working in covenant relationship with humankind, however full and complete, continues to suffer from the weaknesses of human nature. The community united in covenant around only two commandments—to love and believe—is nonetheless fragmenting over what to believe about Christ and how to love one another through the demands of this life. The Elder writes to plead for the best in his community and fights for it to rise to this unity in covenant with God.

The symbolism and language of covenant are thus woven metaphorically throughout the settings and dialogical encounters of the Johannine literature as both Jesus and the Elder challenge those they encounter to accept or reject the relationship Jesus offers. The community to which the Evangelist addressed his Gospel and Letters in order to draw them into the sacred narrative of Scripture is made up of those who have accepted the gift of covenant made possible through belief in Jesus Christ. The Evangelist writes to these children of God so that, despite any experience of suffering and alienation, they can understand themselves as God's new covenant community firmly rooted in the story of the word and action of God in history and forged in the revelation of the glory of God in Jesus Christ. We can now conclude by reflecting upon how the covenant metaphor could be used effectively as the underlying literary fabric of the Evangelist's Scripture for his community and why he might have employed covenant as a guiding storytelling paradigm for his fledgling Christian community in the subtle and nuanced manner he does.

Community and Covenant: Living Life in God's Promise

> John told his story of Jesus for his community. This means that there are two fundamental levels in the communication process sought by the evangelist: (1) the level internal to the text, which portrays the ongoing periods of the narration from the preexistence to the post-existence of Jesus Christ; (2) the level of the Johannine community, external to the text, for which John conceived the story of Jesus in order to lead them to the knowledge and understanding of the saving work of God in Jesus Christ. The interpreter must always keep both levels in mind since John intends his story of Jesus for the community but at the same time binds the community to the story of Jesus.[2]

The narrative level of a story is its content—the sequence of events along a timeline, during which characters interact and develop as a plot unfolds, all of which come to a climax and resolution. The discourse level is the underlying meaning the storyteller wishes to communicate to the audience as a teaching by

---

2. Udo Schnelle, "Recent Views of John's Gospel," *Word & World* 21 (2001): 355–56.

means of that story. Biblical scholar Udo Schnelle's observations above articulate the narrative and discourse levels of the Johannine literature in terms of the gospel story itself and the Evangelist and community for which he composed his version of the good news of God's action in Jesus. Schnelle goes on to argue that the Gospel unfolds "as a post-Easter remembering...that is brought about by the power of the Spirit" and allows the Evangelist to "translate theological insights into narrated history" for his community that concurrently provides them with a direction for the future.[3] This process is what makes the form of the Johannine literature both understandable and effective for its audience.

These observations lead to inquiries on the nature and context of the Johannine community as well as on what the content and goal of the Johannine discourse might be. As far as the Evangelist is concerned, the "who" of his community are the children of God, whatever their ethnic background and identity. This designation is crucial for understanding the intent of the Evangelist but does not fully answer the question of what his educational goal in writing might be. In this vein, Jo-Ann Brant observes:

> Instead of asking, "Who are the children of God?"—
> that is, inquiring about who is in and out—the ques-
> tion that the Fourth Gospel addresses seems to be,
> "What does it mean to be children of God?"...
> Knowledge is a privilege of vantage point. The action of
> the gospel leaves one with the impression that life lived
> as children of God, in truth, as opposed to children of
> a lie, will make clear the competing demands of life.
> Community may risk betrayal. Friendship may demand
> self-sacrifice. The righteous may suffer injustice. The
> certainty that it offers is not a retreat into...false secu-
> rity....Jesus' invitation to Simon Peter to follow him is
> an invitation to give up safety. It is not a denial of suf-
> fering and death. In order to become children of God,
> we must freely step into a world of contingency in

---

3. Ibid., 356.

which we relinquish the security of associations and
make ourselves vulnerable to death.[4]

For the Fourth Evangelist then, living life as the children of God
is thus living a life of truth in the Word of God, but this is not to
say that such a call is easy. This life includes knowledge of God,
love, and community, but it also includes the potentiality and
even eventuality of separation, alienation, and persecution. This
is the Evangelist's particular challenge, and the fruits of persever-
ing as the children of God through this experience are his particular discourse for his readers. But why is this so?

The proposed influences on the religious thought of the
Fourth Evangelist and the context of the Johannine community
have been the focus of much discussion in modern Johannine
scholarship. As a result of twentieth-century archaeological finds
such as the Nag Hammadi library in Egypt and the Dead Sea
Scrolls of Qumran in Israel and following the groundbreaking
work of J. Louis Martyn, a large number of scholars are coming to
agree that the principal background for Johannine thought is the
traditional Judaism of the first century AD. Martyn has famously
described the Gospel of John as a two-level drama.[5] By this, he is
referring to the two levels we introduced above as the narrative
and discourse levels of interpretation. As we read the Johannine
literature, we can envision the drama of the narrative of the good
news of Jesus Christ playing out on a stage. This is the literature's
witness of the events of Jesus' earthly lifetime. At the same time,
there is another stage on which the drama of the community Jesus
forged is playing out. This is how the literature also witnesses to
Jesus' presence in the events experienced by the Johannine
church. This second stage is the discourse level through which the
Evangelist teaches his community and all audiences how and why
they might go on believing.

Israel's Scriptures are the Evangelist's essential literary backdrop, and OT references and themes are woven into both the

---

4. Jo-Ann A. Brant, *Dialogue and Drama: Elements of Greek Tragedy in the Fourth
Gospel* (Peabody: Hendrickson, 2004), 231–32.

5. J. Louis Martyn, *History and Theology in the Fourth Gospel*, 3rd ed. (Louisville:
Westminster John Knox, 2003).

structure of the Johannine literature and the actions and words of Jesus it recounts even when explicit OT citations are lacking. In addition, some of the background of Jesus' thought can be found in the Pharisaic theology of his time, as known from the later rabbinic writings. Furthermore, the thought of Jesus is expressed in a particular theological vocabulary and outlook that is similar to the Jewish Qumran group in first-century Judea. Therefore, behind the Fourth Evangelist's theological conceptualization as well as the Johannine community's developing Christian context lies a complex combination of religious thinking and expression that were current in Judaism during Jesus' lifetime and the generations after his death.

Traditional Judaism also forms a large component of the context of the Johannine community. The opponents of Jesus in the Gospel, identified as "the Jews," likely correlate with the opponents of the Johannine community. These opponents were thus ethnically Jewish people with a fierce commitment to the religion of Israel, specifically as it was being established after the devastations of the first Jewish revolt against Rome (AD 66–70). In AD 70, the Roman army broke through the city walls of Jerusalem, burned the city, and destroyed the second temple. If Judaism was to survive, the rabbis had to reorient the Jewish people away from their lost temple and toward their Scripture and a more homogenous belief system. The rabbis convened at Jamnia, and Martyn argues that eventually this developing orthodoxy included the expulsion of the Christ believers from the synagogues. This is the traumatic experience of the Johannine community of believers in Jesus Christ. The Gospel indicates that these opponents are in a position of authority in the culture of Jewish society. This group casts out the man born blind from the synagogue (9:22, 34), and some of the people are afraid to confess that Jesus is the Messiah lest they too be cast out of the synagogue (12:42). Jesus explicitly warns his disciples that they will be thrown out of the synagogue and even killed by people who understand their own actions as giving praise to God (16:2). Throughout the Gospel, these opponents are portrayed as systematically rejecting Jesus and those who believe and follow him. Expulsion from the synagogue would not have happened during the lifetime of Jesus in the 30s. However, it could have happened to Christ believers in the Evangelist's community at the end of the first century AD. The Fourth Gospel thus arises from a context in which those who believed and confessed that Jesus was the Christ were forcibly excluded from the synagogue. Therefore, however diverse the Johannine community may have been, many of its members were ethnically Jewish and committed to the religion of Israel. As John Ashton has noted so eloquently, one must "recognize in these hot-tempered exchanges the type of family row in which the participants face one another across the room of a house that all have shared and all call home."[6] This is the context into which the Fourth Evangelist writes his Gospel and Letters.

The Gospel according to John states its purpose in the conclusion of the body of the narrative (20:30–31). It is devoted to confirming the faith of those who believe and to giving them further instruction on that faith. Raymond Brown notes that "the Gospel was written in good part to deepen the faith of believers so that they could understand that what they had gained by way of God's life more than made up for what had been lost in their former religious adhesion."[7] What we see in this literature is a strong emphasis on events in Jesus' ministry that foreshadow the sacramental life of the church. The Evangelist speaks to a Christian audience that depends upon baptism and Eucharist for that life. Thus he does not mention these institutions but presupposes them through references to living water and rebirth (John 3:5; 4:10–15; 7:38; 19:34; 1 John 5:6–8), as well as living bread and the wine of the new era (John 2:1–12; 6:31–58; 19:30). Brown further suggests that "John's theology of a divine Word who comes from a heavenly world and expresses himself in the language of this world is a highly sacramental approach if sacraments are understood as external signs that give God's grace."[8] And yet references to these community rituals are descriptive and symbolic, while direct identifications are neither included nor

---

6. John Ashton, *Understanding the Fourth Gospel* (Oxford: Clarendon, 1991), 151.

7. Raymond E. Brown, *An Introduction to the Gospel of John*, ed. Francis J. Moloney, Anchor Yale Bible Reference Library (New York: Doubleday, 2003), 182.

8. Ibid., 230.

necessary. I suggest the Fourth Evangelist is doing something similar with the word "covenant," understood as the metaphor by which God's relationship with humankind is expressed in the language of this world, though arguably for a different reason.

The concept of "witness" in the Johannine literature is an image of the past that combines recollections of Jesus with both the story of the good news and the wealth of Jewish Scripture. The Gospel of John integrates witness to the word of God in the written form of the Torah, the revelation of God in the incarnate form that is Jesus Christ, and the present reality and future hope of his community. Therefore, a corollary to the primary purpose of the Gospel, confirming the faith of the believing community, is connected to the location and cultural milieu of the community and their vision for the future. The larger Greco-Roman world of the community and the literature it produced demanded a narrative that recast the Jewish story of Jesus in the language and style of that world. The expulsion of Christians from the synagogues also necessitated a telling of the story that explained how the one who claimed to be the Jewish Messiah was ultimately rejected by Judaism and became known as Messiah to Christians instead. The Fourth Evangelist consciously incorporated into his writing different attitudes, symbols, and traditions in order to reach out to as many ethnic and religious backgrounds as possible so that his work would have appeal in its new universalizing and transcendent religious world. Ultimately, as a foundational document, the Gospel according to John attempts both to appropriate the traditions of Israel for the emerging faith and to reorient the movement away from the Israelite world of its past and toward the Greco-Roman world of its future.

In many ways, the Evangelist was doing exactly what the rabbis of post-AD 70 Judaism were doing. Facing new crises of life without the temple, for the rabbis, and life beyond the synagogue, for the Evangelist, these community leaders had to reorient their teaching, their literature, and their community (including their terminology). This is why the Evangelist uses the language and symbolism of covenant and the metaphor of fulfillment throughout his writings in the subtle and nuanced manner he does. For some time, the term *covenant* will remain a part of the technical language of the synagogue and post-AD 70 Judaism. Life in the synagogue as well as celebrations of the Jewish feasts and the language and ritual associated with them are part of the Johannine community's past. The Fourth Evangelist is thus taking on the challenge of incorporating his community's need for grounding in God's saving action of the past while reorienting his community members into the larger Greco-Roman world of the future. This process, however painful, is necessary for their survival. Therefore he uses the language and symbolism of covenant while forgoing the term itself in favor of the language of family, knowledge, love, and truth that is also in harmony with the culture and society of their future.

The Fourth Evangelist articulates for his community the continuation of God's covenantal work in creation through the new community founded on truth and belief in the revelation of the Word of God. The Gospel and Letters of John become the lifeline for the fledgling community to find their genealogy in the story of Israel and God's saving covenantal relationship with that chosen people of God. At the same time, the community is able to perceive its future in a world that is the perfection of that story where the revelation of God in Jesus, God's gift of truth, has set all humankind free to accept and believe in the Word of God and to live in covenant relationship with that Word as the true children of God. This, in turn, is also the Evangelist's message for the believing community of all ages: to live and love in the Christ-given power of God's children and to continue sharing that gift God has promised to humanity with the world.

BIBLIOGRAPHY

Ashton, John. *Understanding the Fourth Gospel*. Oxford: Clarendon, 1991.

Brant, Jo-Ann A. *Dialogue and Drama: Elements of Greek Tragedy in the Fourth Gospel*. Peabody: Hendrickson, 2004.

Brown, Raymond E. *An Introduction to the Gospel of John*. Edited by Francis J. Moloney. Anchor Yale Bible Reference Library. New York: Doubleday, 2003.

———. *The Community of the Beloved Disciple: The Life, Loves and Hates of an Individual Church in New Testament Times*. New York: Paulist Press, 1979.

———. "The Passion according to John: Chapters 18 and 19." *Worship* 49 (1975): 130.

Culpepper, R. Alan. "The Pivot of John's Prologue." *New Testament Studies* 27 (1980): 1–31.

Giblin, Charles H. "Confrontations in John 18, 1–27." *Biblica* 65 (1984): 215.

Hooker, Morna. *Beginnings: Keys That Open the Gospels*. Harrisburg, PA: Trinity Press International, 1997.

———. *Endings: Invitations to Discipleship*. Peabody, MA: Hendrickson, 2003.

Malatesta, Edward. "Interiority and Covenant: A Study of εἶναι ἐν and μένειν ἐν in the First Letter of Saint John." *Analecta biblica* 69. Rome: Biblical Institute Press, 1978.

Martyn, J. Louis. *History and Theology in the Fourth Gospel*. 3rd ed. Louisville: Westminster John Knox, 2003.

Meeks, Wayne A. "The Prophet-King: Moses Traditions and the Johannine Christology." *Novum Testamentum Supplements* 14. Leiden: Brill, 1967.

Moloney, Francis J. *The Gospel of John*. Sacra Pagina 4. Collegeville, MN: Liturgical Press, 1998.

Schnelle, Udo. "Recent Views of John's Gospel." *Word & World* 21 (2001): 355–56.